SPOKEN
ITALIAN

SECOND EDITION

SPOKEN ITALIAN
for students and travelers

Charles Speroni

University of California, Los Angeles

Charles E. Kany

D. C. HEATH AND COMPANY

Lexington, Massachusetts   Toronto

PREFACE

Much time has gone by since the first edition of *Spoken Italian for Students and Travelers,* but it has nevertheless shown a remarkable staying power. Because of this, and because of the constantly increasing interest in the study of Italian in colleges and high schools, as well as in extension and evening classes aimed at the general public, both the publisher and I felt that an updated edition of *Spoken Italian* should be published.

In preparing this new edition I first eliminated a few conversations that seemed no longer appropriate—for example, getting a visa at the Italian Consulate—and replaced them with more appropriate ones—for example, renting a car. Basically, however, the original plan has been retained. Also, after much thought I decided to retain the diacritical marks to indicate open *e*'s and *o*'s and voiced *s*'s and *z*'s throughout the text and Appendix; I have not used them in the exercises at the end of the book, which consist entirely of questions that will generally be asked by the teacher. It is well known that Italians do not agree in every instance on open and closed *e*'s and *o*'s, or even on voiced and unvoiced *s*'s and *z*'s; the fact remains, however, that in doubtful cases the Tuscan usage still prevails, as witnessed by all standard Italian dictionaries.

Spoken Italian for Students and Travelers deviates considerably from the traditional foreign language textbook, both in structure and purpose. Its purpose is to offer easy but adequate conversational Italian to students of the language and to travelers and tourists in Italy. The book may be considered a basic conversational text not only for beginners with no knowledge of Italian, but also for those who already possess a foundation. A skeleton grammar is appended for the benefit of those who may wish to consult it. To this end, references will be found throughout the text corresponding to explanatory paragraphs in the Appendix, which also contains the conjugation of the more common irregular verbs, a conversion table of the metric system, and examples of business and personal correspondence. An index to the Appendix is also provided.

The conversations have been carefully selected to meet the ordinary requirements of the traveler in his daily life and have likewise been graded as to difficulty of expression. The English translation given for each Italian sentence is a time-saving device particularly helpful for self-instruction.

If composition is required, students may prepare a similar dialogue with variations. Furthermore, the teacher may formulate his or her own questions in Italian concerning the material under study. With this in mind, at the suggestion of fellow teachers of Italian, I have added at the end of the book a series of sample questions based on the text. Again, each student may memorize a few dialogues. Any two who have thus selected the same dialogue could then recite it together before the class, with appropriate action and gestures.

Charles Speroni

CONTENTS

3   In giro per l'Italia

4   Vita quotidiana

5   Il viaggio finisce

ITALIA POLITICA

PRONUNCIATION

The *approximate*[1] English equivalents are as follows:

I. Vowels (all are short and clear):

a as in *a*h!

e sometimes as in th*ey* (without the final *i* glide sound of English); sometimes like *e* in m*e*t. The latter sound is called the "open" *e* and, as an aid to the student, is written ɛ in this book.

o sometimes as in *o*pen (without the final *u* glide sound of English); sometimes like *o* in n*o*rth. The latter sound is called the "open" *o* and, as an aid to the student, is written ɔ in this book.

i as in mach*i*ne

u as in r*u*le

II. Consonants (those not mentioned here are *approximately* as in English):

c before **a, o, u** as in *c*at but softer

c before **e, i** as in *ch*in[2]

---

[1] Only approximate sounds can be discussed here. Imitation should be practiced.
[2] When **ci, gi,** and **gli** are followed by **a, o, u,** the **i** (unless stressed) is silent and merely indicates that the **c, g,** and **gl** have a palatal sound.

ch   (it occurs only before **e** or **i**) as in *c*at but softer

d   approximately like the *d* in *d*o but tongue touches upper teeth

g   before **a, o, u** as in *g*o

g   before **e, i** as in *g*em[1]

gh   (it occurs only before **e** or **i**) as in *g*o

gli   approximately as in mi*lli*on, but the **ll** begins the syllable[1]

gn   approximately as in ca*ny*on, but the **gn** begins the syllable

h   is silent

l   farther forward in mouth than in English

p   as in English, but softer

qu   as in *qu*iet

r   is pronounced with a vibration of the tongue against upper teeth

s   sometimes as in *s*ee; sometimes (always when preceding **m, n, d, b, v, g,** and **l**) as in ro*s*e. The latter sound is called the voiced *s* and, as an aid to the student, is italicized in this book.

t   approximately as in English, but tip of tongue touches edge of upper front teeth, and no escaping of breath is heard.

sc   before **a, o, u**, as in *sk*etch

sc   before **e, i** as in *sh*ot

sch   (occurs only before **e** or **i**) as in *sk*etch

---

[1] When **ci, gi,** and **gli** are followed by **a, o, u,** the **i** (unless stressed) is silent and merely indicates that the **c, g,** and **gl** have a palatal sound.

z sometimes like *ts* in be*ts*; sometimes like *ds* in be*ds*. The latter sound is called the "voiced" **z** and, as an aid to the student, is italicized in this book.

III. Double Consonants
Double consonants are pronounced much more forcefully than single consonants. With double **f, l, m, n, r, s,** and **v,** the sound is prolonged; with double **b, c, d, g, p, t,** the explosion is held back twice as long as for a single consonant. Double **zz** is pronounced almost the same as single **z.**

IV. Stress
The stressed vowel of an Italian word is indicated only if it is final (**città**). The stress of other words must be learned. To be sure, most words stress the next-to-the-last syllable.

To facilitate pronunciation, we have in this book used certain orthographic devices. The student will have no difficulty if he observes the following: Stress the syllable containing an accented vowel (**città**), an open **e** (**lɛttera**), an open **o** (**nɔtte**), or any other vowel when italicized (**ad*a*gio**); in all other words, stress the next-to-the-last vowel.

V. Apostrophe
The apostrophe is generally used to indicate the dropping of the final vowel: **l'amico** instead of **lo amico**; **l'autom*ɔ*bile** instead of **la autom*ɔ*bile**; **d'ɔro** instead of **di ɔro**.

VI. Syllabification
1. A single consonant goes with the following vowel: **ca-sa, vo-le-re.**
2. Double consonants are divided: **bɛl-lo, ros-so.**
3. Two consonants, the first of which is **l, m, n,** or **r,** are divided: **an-da-re, al-bɛr-go.**

4. Otherwise, a combination of two consonants belongs to the following syllable: **ve-sti-re**, **pro-gre-di-re**.
5. The first of three consonants, except **s**, goes with the preceding syllable: **al-tro**, **den-tro**, **sɛm-pre**. But: **dɛ-stra**.
6. Combinations of unstressed **i** or **u** with a vowel are never divided: **piɛ-no**, **nuɔ-vo**.

Preparativi per un viaggio in Italia

Preparing for a Trip to Italy

Scambiando saluti

Exchanging Greetings

Buɔn giorno
> *Good morning.*

Buɔn giorno.
> *Good morning.*

Come sta Lɛi?[1]
> *How are you?*

Bɛne, grazie. E Lɛi?
> *Very well, thank you. And you?*

Così, così.[2] Non stɔ trɔppo bɛne.
> *So so. I'm not too well.*

Mi dispiace.
> *I'm sorry (lit. "it displeases me").*

Grazie.
> *Thank you.*

Arrivederla (*or* Arrivederci).
> *Good-bye (lit. "I'll see you again.").*

A domani.
> *See you tomorrow.*

---

[1]**come sta Lɛi?** = **come sta?** [2] **così, così** = **non c'è male,** *not bad* = **si tira avanti,** *one manages to get along.*

Buɔna sera, sign*or*[3] Bianchi.
> *Good evening, Mr. Bianchi.*

Buɔna sera, signora.
> *Good evening, Mrs.* ——.

Sta bɛne la[4] signora Bianchi?
> *Is Mrs. Bianchi well?*

Sì, gr*a*zie. Sta molto bɛne.
> *Yes, thank you. She's very well.*

E come sta Giovanni?
> *And how is John?*

Anche lui sta bɛne, gr*a*zie.
> *He's well too, thank you.*

Allora tutto va[5] bɛne.
> *Then everything is fine.*

Arrivederla, signora.
> *Good-bye, Mrs.* ——.

Buɔna sera.
> *Good evening.*

NƆTE

1.   **buɔna sera** can also mean *good afternoon;* **buɔna nɔtte** = *good night.* **buɔn giorno** and **buɔna sera** are used when taking leave and also as a greeting. See § 16*b*.

2.   In familiar usage: **come va?** (*how goes it?*); also **ciao!** *hello!* (**ciao** also means *good-bye*); **che c'ɛ̀ di nuɔvo?** *what's new?* or *what's up?* For forms of address see § 33.

---

[3] Before a name, **signore** drops the final **e**. § 14*b*. (This and similar references indicate corresponding paragraphs of the grammatical Appendix. Such references are made throughout the book for the benefit of those who wish to consult the grammar.)   [4] In indirect address titles are preceded by the definite article. § 2*f*.   [5] Third person singular of the irregular verb **andare**, *to go.* § 75 (1).

3.   **arrivederla** (or **arrivederci**) = **ci vediamo** (more familiar). **Arrivederci** is more familiar than **arrivederla** when addressing one person; it is used generally when saying good-bye to two or more people. In taking leave, **addio** and **ciao** are also used: **addio** with the meaning *good-bye*; **ciao**, which is more familiar, with the meaning *so long, etc.*

4.   **signore, signora, signorina** (*Mr., Mrs., Miss*) are often used in direct address where in English the corresponding form is often either omitted or followed by the person's name.

5.   **lui**, *he*; **lɛi**, *she*; **loro**, *they* are the stressed forms of **egli, ella**, and **essi**, respectively; they are used more and more as subject pronouns in place of the unstressed forms.

Parla italiano Lɛi?

Do You Speak Italian?

Buɔn giorno.
> *Good morning.*

Buɔn giorno.
> *Good morning.*

È[1] italiano (-a) Lɛi?
> *Are you (an) Italian?*

Sì, signore. E Lɛi?
> *Yes, sir. And you?*

Io sono[1] americano (-a).
> *I'm (an) American.*

Parla italiano Lɛi?
> *Do you speak Italian?*

Sì, un pɔ'.[2]
> *Yes, a little.*

Lɛi parla inglese.
> *You speak English.*

Sì. Anche Lɛi parla inglese?
> *Yes. Do you speak English too?*

Nɔ, io non parlo inglese.
> *No, I don't speak English.*

---

[1] From **ɛssere,** *to be.* § 75 (14).   [2] **pɔ'** is the shortened form of **pɔco.**

Peccato!
>Too bad.

È vero.
>It really is.

Arrivederla.
>Good-bye.

Arrivederla.
>Good-bye.

NOTE

1. Other adjectives of nationality are **tedesco (tedesca)**, *German*; **russo (russa)**, *Russian*; **inglese**, *English*; **francese**, *French*; etc. See also § 79.

2. In questions the subject frequently follows the verb.

3. Adjectives agree in gender with the person qualified. A woman says **sono italiana, russa, tedesca**, etc. If the adjective ends in **-e**, however, no change is necessary. See §§ 9, 10, 4*a*.

Ha un fiamm*i*fero?

Do You Have a Match?

Scu*s*i,[1] ha[2] un fiamm*i*fero?
Excuse me, do you have a match?

Non capisco. Parli[1] ad*a*gio.
I don't understand. Speak slowly.

Fiamm*i*fero . . . sigaretta. Capisce?
Match . . . cigarette. Do you understand?

Ah, sì. Capisco. Certamente. Ɛcco.
Oh, yes. I understand. Sure. Here (you are).

Gr*a*zie.
Thank you.

Prɛgo.[3]
You're welcome.

Pɔsso [4] offrirle [5] una sigaretta?
(May I offer you a) cigarette?

Gr*a*zie. Io fumo soltanto la pipa.
No thanks. I only smoke a (lit. "the") pipe.

Dov'ɛ una tabaccheria?
Where is a tobacco shop?

---

[1] **scu*s*i** and **parli** are the command forms of **scu*s*are** and **parlare** corresponding to **Lɛi.** The command forms of **Lɛi** and **Loro** come from the present subjunctive. §§ 69, 71.   [2] From **avere,** *to have.* § 75 (3).   [3] **prɛgo**=**di niɛnte.**   [4] **pɔsso** is a form of the irregular verb **potere,** *to be able to, can, may.* § 75 (21).   [5] § 34.

Qu*i* all'[6] *a*ngolo.
> *Here at the corner.*

Des*i*dero comprare un pacchetto di sigarette. Arrivederla.
> *I want to buy a pack of cigarettes. Good-bye.*

Bu*o*n giorno.
> *Good-bye.*

NOTE

1. **grazie** can mean *no thank you* or *thank you.*

2. Other vocabulary: **accendino,** *lighter*; **portacenere** *m.*, *ashtray.*

---

[6] **a + l' = all'** . § 18.

Una lεttera

A Letter

Ha carta da[1] lεttere?
Do you have writing paper?

Sì. Ɛcco la carta ed εcco le buste.
Yes. Here's the paper and here are the envelopes.

Vɔglio[2] scrivere alcune[3] lεttere.
I want to write some letters.

Ha una penna?
Do you have a pen?

Sì, εccola.
Yes, here it is.

Ha francobolli?[4]
Do you have stamps?

Sì. Che francobolli vuɔle?[2]
Yes. What stamps do you want?

Cinque francobolli per pɔsta aεrea.
Five airmail stamps.

Ɛccoli.
Here they are.

Lεi è molto gentile.
You're very kind.

---

[1] § 62*b*.   [2] **vɔglio, vuɔle** are forms of the irregular verb **volere,** *to want.* § 75 (40).
[3] § 19*b*.   [4] § 19*c*.

Grazie. La buca per le lettere è di fronte.
> *Not at all (lit. "thank you"). The mailbox is across the street (lit. "facing here").*

Mille grazie.
> *Many thanks (lit. "a thousand thanks").*

NOTE

1.   Before an *e*, **e** usually becomes **ed**.

2.   Direct object pronouns follow **ɛcco**, *here is, here are, there is, there are*: **ɛccomi**, *here I am*; **ɛccola**, *here (there) she is*; **ɛccoli (ɛccole)**, *here (there) they are*, etc.

La famiglia

The Family

Ha scritto[1] alla[2] Sua[3] famiglia?
  Have you written to your family?

Sì, hɔ scritto due lɛttere.
  Yes, I've written two letters.

A chi ha scritto?
  Who have you written to?

A mio[4] padre, a mia madre, e a Paolo.
  (To) my father, my mother, and Paul.

Scrive molte lɛttere Lɛi?
  Do you write many letters?

Scrivo spesso ai[2] miɛi genitori.
  I write often to my parents.

Dov'ɛ il Suo amico Paolo ora?
  Where's your friend Paul now?
Ɛ a[5] Nuɔva Yɔrk.
  He's in New York.

Anche Suo fratɛllo ɛ a Nuɔva Yɔrk?
  Is your brother in New York, too?

Nɔ, lui [6] ɛ a Napoli.
  No, he's in Naples.

---

[1] Irregular past participle of **scrivere**, *to write*. § 75 (30).   [2] **a + la = alla; a + i = ai.** § 18.   [3] § 25*a*.   [4] § 25*b*.   [5] § 63*b*.   [6] § 39*a*.

Che cosa fa[7] Paolo a Nuova York?
What's Paul doing in New York?

Studia medicina.
He's studying medicine.

NOTE

1. **dove,** *where,* frequently becomes **dov'** before a vowel.

2. Italian repeats a preposition in a list, while English often does not (e.g., **a mio padre, a mia madre.** . .).

---

[7] From **fare,** *to do, make.* § 75 (15).

Il tεmpo

The Weather

Che tεmpo fa?
> *How's the weather (lit. "what weather does it make")?*

Fa freddo. Fa molto freddo.
> *It's cold. It's very cold.*

Perchè ὲ invεrno.
> *Because it's winter.*

Fa sεmpre brutto tεmpo nell'invεrno?[1]
> *Is the weather always bad in winter?*

Quaṣi sεmpre. Spesso nevica.[2]
> *Almost always. Often it snows.*

E qualche vɔlta c'ὲ[3] la nebbia.
> *And sometimes there's fog.*

E tira molto vεnto.
> *And it's very windy (lit. "much wind blows").*

Nella primavεra fa bεl tεmpo.
> *In spring the weather is fine.*

Perɔ piɔve molto.
> *But it rains a good deal.*

E c'ὲ molto sole.
> *And there's a lot of sun.*

---

[1] **nell'invεrno**＝**in invεrno**＝**d'invεrno; nella primavεra**＝**in primavεra**＝**di prima-vεra,** etc.   [2] **nevica**＝**fiɔcca; cade la neve,** *the snow falls.*   [3] **ci,** *there,* usually becomes **c'** before an **e** or an **i.**

Nell'estate fa molto caldo.
In summer it's very warm.

L'autunno è la migliore[4] stagione.
Autumn is the best season.

Perchè fa caldo il giorno.[5]
Because it's warm during the day.

E fa fresco la nɔtte.
And it's cool at night.

NɔTE

Fa bɛl (buɔn) tɛmpo, *the weather is fine;* **fa brutto (cattivo) tɛmpo,** *the weather is bad.* See § 67*b*.

---

[4] § 20*a*.   [5] **il giorno (la nɔtte)＝di giorno (di nɔtte).**

L'ora

The Time

Che ora è? (or Che ore sono?)
> *What time (lit. "hour") is it?*

È l'una (in punto).
> *It's one o'clock (sharp).*

È l'una e cinque (minuti).
> *It's five minutes past one.*

È l'una e un quarto.
> *It's a quarter past one.*

È l'una e venti.
> *It's twenty minutes after one.*

È l'una e mezza (or È l'una e trenta).
> *It's half past one.*

Sono le due meno venti (or Mancano venti minuti alle due).
> *It's twenty minutes to two (lit. "two less twenty").*

Sono le due meno un quarto (or Manca un quarto alle due).
> *It's a quarter to two.*

Sono le due.
> *It's two o'clock.*

Sono le tre, etc.
> *It's three o'clock, etc.*

NOTE
When indicating the time of trains, buses, theatrical performances, office hours, etc., it is customary to continue counting after twelve noon to twenty-four (midnight). **Alle quindici** (*fifteen*) = *at three P.M.*, etc. This official practice, however, is not very common in ordinary conversation.

La presentazione

The Introduction

Le presento[1] il mio amico (la mia amica).
May I introduce (lit. "I introduce") my friend.

Piacere![2]
How do you do (lit. "it's a pleasure").

Piacere!
How do you do.

Mi permetta[3] di presentarmi: io sono Carlo Moretti.
Allow me to introduce myself: I am Charles Moretti.

E io Remo Abate.
And I (am) Remo Abate.

(Accomiatandosi) Felice di aver[4] fatto[5] la Sua conoscenza.
(Taking leave) Nice to have met you (lit. "happy to have made your acquaintance").

Il piacere è stato[6] mio.
And I you (lit. "the pleasure was mine").

---

[1] **Le presento** = **mi permetta di presentarle;** for position of object pronouns see §§ 34, 35.   [2] **piacere** = **piacere di fare la Sua conoscenza,** *I am pleased to make your acquaintance.*   [3] Present subjunctive of **permettere**, *to permit, let.* § 71. [4] §14*a*.   [5] Past participle of **fare**. § 75 (15).   [6] **è stato**, *has been.* §§ 75 (14), 70.

Va in Italia?

Are You Going to Italy?

Buɔn giorno, signor Brown.
> *Good morning, Mr. Brown.*

Buɔn giorno. Come va?[1]
> *Good morning. How are you?*

Mɛglio[2] di[3] iɛri[4].
> *Better than yesterday.*

Mi fa piacere.[5]
> *That's good (lit. "it does me pleasure").*

Che c'ɛ di nuɔvo?
> *What's new (with you)?*

Dɛvo[6] studiare l'italiano.[7]
> *I have to study Italian.*

Ma Lɛi già lo parla bɛne.
> *But you already speak it well.*

Macchè! Vɔglio fare[8] un viaggio.
> *Nonsense! I want to take a trip.*

Dove?
> *Where?*

In[9] Italia.
> *To Italy.*

---

[1] From **andare,** *to go.* § 75 (1).   [2] **mɛglio,** *better, best.* § 31.   [3] § 22.   [4] **iɛri,**
yesterday.   [5] **mi fa piacere** = **sono contɛnto.**   [6] From **dovere,** *to have to, must.*
§ 75 (13).   [7] **l'italiano,** *Italian.* § 2e.   [8] **fare un viaggio,** *to take a trip.*   [9] § 63a.

Beato Lɛi!
> *Aren't you lucky!*

È vero. Ora, però, dɛvo studiare la lingua.
> *I certainly am (lit. "it's true"). But now I have to study the language.*

Ma non la studiò[10] alla scuɔla?
> *But didn't you study it in school?*

Sì, molti anni fa.[11]
> *Yes, many years ago.*

Quanti anni fa?
> *How many years ago?*

Cinque o sɛi.
> *Five or six.*

E l'ha dimenticata?[12]
> *And you've forgotten it?*

Hɔ dimenticato tutto.
> *I've forgotten everything.*

Allora non dɛve[6] pɛrdere tɛmpo.
> *Then you mustn't waste (lit. "lose") (any) time.*

NOTE

1. Other expressions of time are: ɔggi, *today*; **domani,** *tomorrow*; **dopo domani,** *the day after tomorrow*; **iɛr l'altro** or **l'altro iɛri,** *the day before yesterday.*

2. Other expressions for taking trips are: **fare un viaggio per mare, per tɛrra, in trɛno,** or **in ferrovia, in aeroplano, in automɔbile,** etc., *to take an ocean trip, a trip on land, a train trip, a plane trip, a car trip,* etc.

---

[10] **studiò,** preterite of **studiare,** *to study.* §§ 69, 45c.   [11] **fa,** third person singular of the present of the irregular verb **fare,** *to do, make.* § 75 (15).   [12] **dimenticare,** *to forget.* §§ 43a, 70.

Buon viaggio

Have a Good Trip

Buona sera.
> *Good afternoon.*

Buona sera.
> *Good afternoon.*

Come vanno[1] le cose?
> *How are things going?*

Al solito.
> *As usual.*

Studia molto?
> *Are you studying much?*

Sì. Sto ripassando[2] la grammatica.
> *Yes. I'm reviewing the grammar.*

Felicitazioni![3] Quando parte?[4]
> *Congratulations! When do you leave?*

Presto. Il mese prossimo.
> *Very soon. Next month.*

Va[1] in piroscafo o in aeroplano?
> *Are you going by boat or by plane?*

In aeroplano. Ci sono molti voli diretti da Nuova York a Roma.
> *By airplane. There are a lot of direct flights from New York to Rome.*

---

[1] **va, vanno,** irregular forms of **andare,** *to go.* §75 (1).   [2] **ripassare,** *to review.* § 72.   [3] **felicitazioni!** *congratulations!* § 81.   [4] **partire,** *to leave.*

Viaggerà⁵ solo?

Will you be traveling alone?

Credo di sì, ma in Italia ho degli⁶ amici.

I think so, but I have some friends in Italy.

Se non ci rivediamo, buon viaggio.

If I don't see you again (lit. "if we don't see each other again"), have a nice trip.

Grazie.

Thank you.

NOTE

1. The present tense is often used as a future (e.g., **parte**). See § 45*a*.

2. Compare **il mese prossimo** with **il mese venturo** or **che viene**; **il mese passato** (or **scorso**), *last month*; **la settimana ventura**, *next week*; **l'anno passato**, *last year*, etc.

3. Other means of transportation are: **aviogetto**, *jet*; **elicottero**, *helicopter*.

4. Compare **credo di sì** with **credo di no**, *I think not*; also with **dire di sì**, *to say yes*, **dire di no**, *to say no*; and with **rispondere di sì**, *to reply in the affirmative*, **rispondere di no**, *to reply in the negative*.

---

⁵ **viaggiare**, *to travel*. § 73*b*.   ⁶ § 19*a*.

L'agenzia di viaggi

The Travel Agency

Buon giorno, signore (signora, signorina), che cosa[1] desidera?
> *Good morning, sir, what can I do for you (lit. "what do you wish")?*

Desidero fare un viaggio in Italia.
> *I want to take a trip to Italy.*

Benissimo.[2] Quando intende partire?
> *Fine. When do you plan to leave?*

La settimana prossima. Giovedì.
> *Next week. On Thursday.*

Giovedì l'Alitalia ha due voli: uno alle diciotto e uno alle diciannove e trenta.
> *On Thursday Alitalia has two flights: one at 6:00 P.M. (lit. "at 18 hours"), and one at 7:30 P.M. (lit. "19:30 hours").*

Preferisco partire alle diciannove e trenta.
> *I prefer to leave at 7:30 P.M.*

Benissimo. Arriverà a Roma venerdì alle dieci di mattina.[3]
> *O.K. You will arrive in Rome on Friday at 10:00 A.M.*

Vuole viaggiare in prima classe o in classe turistica?
> *Do you want to go first class or tourist?*

In classe turistica.
> *Tourist.*

---

[1] che cosa?=cosa?=che?, *what?*   [2] § 24.   [3] di mattina=antimeridiane (A.M.), di sera=pomeridiane (P.M.).

Il Suo passaporto è in regola?
Is your passport in order?

Sì, sì.
Yes.

Quanto tempo intende restare in Italia?
How long do you intend to stay in Italy?

Quarantadue giorni. È un viaggio di piacere.
Forty-two days. It's a pleasure trip.

Paga il biglietto in contanti, con un assegno personale o con
una carta di credito?
Will you pay for your ticket with cash, a personal check,
or a credit card?

Con un assegno personale.
With a personal check.

Benissimo. Ecco il Suo biglietto.
Fine. Here is your ticket.

Grazie. E questo è l'assegno.
Thank you. And this is my check.

Mille grazie. Buon viaggio e buon divertimento.
Thank you very much. Have a nice trip and a good time.

NOTE

The English "on" before days of the week is usually not
translated. **I giorni della settimana sono** (*the days of the week are*):
lunedì (*Monday*), **martedì** (*Tuesday*), **mercoledì** (*Wednesday*),
giovedì (*Thursday*), **venerdì** (*Friday*), **sabato** (*Saturday*), **domenica**
(*Sunday*).

Il viaggio in aeroplano

The Airplane Trip

■ **In volo**   *In Flight*

Ɛccomi all'aeropɔrto. Quel tassì ha fatto prɛsto, ma non c'ɛ̀ tɛmpo da pɛrdere.

> *Here I am at the airport. That taxi got here fast (lit. "has done quickly"), but there's no time to lose.*

Signore, qu*i* ɛ̀ proibito fumare.

> *Sir, no smoking is allowed here (lit. "smoking is forbidden here").*

Scu*s*i, non avevo veduto l'avvi*s*o. Dov'ɛ̀ l'aeroplano per Roma?

> *I'm sorry (lit. "excuse me"), I hadn't seen the sign. Where is the plane for Rome?*

Laggiù a sinistra. Il passapɔrto e il biglietto per favore.

> *Down there on the left. Your (lit. "the") passport and your (lit. "the") ticket please.*

Ɛccoli. E questo ɛ̀ il mio bag*a*glio: una val*i*gia e un pɔrta-*a*biti.

> *Here they are. And this is my luggage: one suitcase and one garment bag.*

Il peso va bɛne. Non c'ɛ̀ bag*a*glio in eccedɛnza. Ɛcco il biglietto e il passapɔrto. S'affretti[1] perchè l'aɛreo sta per partire.

> *The weight is all right. There is no excess baggage. Here are your ticket and passport. Hurry up because the airplane is about to leave.*

[1] § 74.

Salga[2] pure[3] a bordo, signore.
Go right on board, sir.

Che posto Le hanno assegnato, signore?
What seat have they given you, sir?

Il numero 29B (ventinove bi)
Number 29B.

È questo.
It's this one.

Grazie.
Thank you.

Si allaccino la cintura di sicurezza perchè stiamo per decollare.
Fasten your seat belts because we are about to take off.

Che[4] decollo perfetto! Sembra impossibile ma siamo già ad alta quota.
What a perfect take-off! It seems impossible, but we are already at a high altitude.

(Al signore vicino) Quando servono il pranzo?
(To the man next to him) When are they going to serve dinner?

Fra pochi minuti.
In a few minutes.

Meno male; io ho già fame.
That's good (lit. "less bad"); I'm hungry already.

Ahi! Che è stato? Un vuoto d'aria?
Wow! What was that? An air pocket?

Macchè! I vuoti d'aria non esistono.
Not at all! There's no such thing as air pockets (lit. "air pockets don't exist").

Allora che succede?[5]
What's the matter then?

---

[2] From **salire.** § 75 (27).   [3] **pure** gives permission.   [4] § 41.   [5] **che succede** (or **accade**)? *what's happening?* or *what's the matter?*

Sono le corrɛnti d'*a*ria che c*au*sano questi tuffi.
> *It's the air currents that cause these jolts (lit. "dives").*

Mi fanno male gli orecchi.[6]
> *My ears hurt.*

Ɛ l'altit*u*dine. A vɔlte succɛde, anche se nell'aɛreo la pressione è controllata.
> *It's the altitude. It happens at times, even if the plane is pressurized (lit. "the pressure is controlled").*

Lo *s*badigliare[7] a vɔlte giova.
> *Sometimes yawning helps.*

Ɛ vero. Mi sento[8] mɛglio.
> *It's true. I feel better.*

Bɛ', è tardi. Il volo è lungo, e ora vɔglio dormire un pɔ'.
> *Well, it's late. It's a long flight, and now I want to sleep a while.*

Ɛ un' ɔttima[9] idɛa.
> *That's an excellent idea.*

NOTE

1. The opposite of **laggiù** is **lassù**.

2. Other expressions with **pure** are: **entri pure**, *come right in*; **parli pure**, *speak up*; etc.

3. A stewardess might also say: **questo posto è occupato (libero)**, *this seat is occupied (free)*.

4. A plane passenger might also say: **hɔ gli orecchi tappati**, *my ears are stopped up*.

5. Other expressions with **sentirsi** are: **mi sɛnto male (stanco, triste, allegro)**, *I feel ill (tired, sad, happy)*; **sɛnto caldo (freddo)**, *I feel warm (cold)*.

---

[6] lit. "my ears are hurting me," § 2*h*.   [7] §§ 2*j*, 55*b*.   [8] **sentirsi**, *to feel*.   [9] § 24*a*.

2

Soggiorno a Roma

Sojourn in Rome

L'atterraggio e la dogana

Landing and Customs

Quelle montagne[1] coperte di neve sono le Alpi. Fra un'ora atterreremo.
> *Those snow-covered mountains are the Alps. In an hour we'll land.*

Caffè o caffellatte, signore?
> *Black coffee or coffee with milk, sir?*

Grazie, caffè con zucchero.
> *Thank you, black coffee with sugar.*

Eccoci all'aeroporto di Roma.
> *Here we are at the Rome airport.*

Il mio passaporto e i miei bagagli sono pronti.
> *My passport and bags are ready.*

(Doganiere) Ha qualche cosa da[2] dichiarare?
> *(Customs Officer) Do you have anything to declare?*

No.
> *No.*

Ha tabacco, sigarette?
> *Do you have tobacco, cigarettes?*

Solamente dieci pacchetti di sigarette.
> *Only ten packs of cigarettes.*

Che cosa c'è in questa valigia?
> *What's in this suitcase?*

---

[1] **la montagna** = **il monte**, *mountain.*   [2] § 62*b*.

Effɛtti personali: *a*biti, cam*i*cie...
Personal effects: suits, shirts. . . .

Ben*i*ssimo. L'uscita è a dɛstra.
O.K. The exit is on the right.

Ɛcco l'uff*i*cio di c*a*mbio.
Here is the (foreign) exchange office.

Quanti dɔllari des*i*dera cambiare, signore?
How many dollars do you wish to change, sir?

Questi tre assegni per viaggiatori.
These three traveler's checks.

(Facchino)[3] Signore, qu*i* c'è l'*a*utobus che va in città.
(Porter) Sir, here's the bus that goes to the city.

Preferisco prɛndere un tassì.
I prefer to take a taxi.

NƆTE

1.   Other useful vocabulary suggested by **montagne**: **catena di montagne** (or **monti**), *mountain chain*; **la vetta**, *the peak*.

2.   Other useful vocabulary suggested by **sigarette**: **porta-sigarette** *m.*, *cigarette case*; **borsa da tabacco**, *tobacco pouch*; **bocchino**, *cigar(ette) holder*; **contrabbandiɛre**, *smuggler*; **fare il contrabbando**, *to smuggle*.

3.   The opposite of **uscita** is **entrata**.

4.   The opposite of **a destra** is **a sinistra**. Other useful directions are: **sɛmpre diritto**, *straight ahead*; **avanti**, *ahead, forward*; **indiɛtro**, *back*.

---

[3] **facchino = portabagagli**, *m.*

Il tassì

The Taxi

È libero?
> *Are you free?*

Sì, signore. Dove vuole andare?
> *Yes, sir. Where do you want to go?*

Mi porti[1] all'Hotel Imperiale. Questi sono i miei bagagli.
> *Take me to the Hotel Imperiale. These are my bags.*

Benissimo.[2]
> *O.K.*

Lei corre troppo.
> *You're driving too fast.*

Il signore non vuole arrivare al più presto possibile?
> *Don't you (lit. "doesn't the gentleman") want to arrive as soon as possible?*

Sì, ma voglio arrivare sano e salvo.
> *Yes, but I want to arrive safe and sound.*

Non si preoccupi, noi tassisti[3] siamo abituati al traffico.
> *Don't worry, we taxi drivers are accustomed to traffic.*

Sì, ma non si sa[4] mai.[5]
> *Yes, but one never knows.*

Eccoci alle porte della città.
> *Here we are at the city gates.*

---

[1] Present subjunctive of **portare**. §§ 71, 35.   [2] § 24.   [3] 7b   [4] § 59b   [5] From **sapere**, § 75 (28); 32b.

È lontano l'hotɛl?
> *Is the hotel far?*

Non trɔppo.
> *Not too far.*

Che piazza è questa?
> *What square is this?*

È Piazza Barberini. Ɛcco l'hotɛl.
> *It's Barberini Square. Here is the hotel.*

Sì. Ɛccoci giunti.[6]
> *Yes. Here we are.*

(Scendɛndo dal tassì) Quanto segna il tassametro?
> (*Getting out of the taxi*) *How much does the meter read?*

Ɔtto mila lire.[7]
> *Eight thousand lire.*

Ɛcco. E questo è per Lɛi.
> *Here you are. And this is for you.*

Grazie. Buɔn giorno.
> *Thank you. Have a good day.*

NɔTE
> The opposite of è **lontano** is è **vicino**.

---

[6] Past participle of **giungere,** *to arrive.* § 75 (16).   [7]§ 76.

L'albɛrgo

The Hotel

Ha una camera a un lɛtto?
Do you have a single room?

Sì ,signore. A che piano la preferisce?
Yes, sir. On what floor would you prefer it?

Non impɔrta, ma vorrɛi[1] una camera estɛrna.
It doesn't matter, but I'd like an outside room.

Ben*i*ssimo. Il n*u*mero 48 (quarantɔtto) è dispon*i*bile e dà[2]
sulla strada.
All right. Number 48 is vacant and faces the street.

Vuɔle mostr*a*rmela?[3]
Would you show it to me?

Con piacere. Saliamo[4] in ascensore. Di qu*i* . . . è questa.
Come Le pare?
Of course (lit. "with pleasure"). We'll go up in the elevator.
This way . . . It's this one. How do you like it?

È un pɔ' p*i*ccola, ma non impɔrta.
It's a little small, but it doesn't matter.

Come vede, di giorno c'è molta luce.
As you can see, during the day there is a lot of light.

C'è il bagno?
Is there a bath?

---

[1] Conditional of **volere**, *to want* § 75 (40).   [2] From dare, *to give.* § 75 (10).
[3] §§ 34, 36.   [4] § 45*a*.

(Apre una pɔrta) È questo. C'è la vasca, la dɔccia e il gabinetto.
(Opens a door) Here it is. There's a tub, a shower, and a toilet.

C'è l'aria condizionata?
Is it air conditioned?

Nɔ, ma qui non fa mai trɔppo caldo.
No, but here it is never too hot.

Va bɛne. La prɛndo.[4]
All right. I'll take it.

Scendiamo.
Let's go down.

Per favore mi dia[5] il passapɔrto e riɛmpia questo mɔdulo di registrazione col Suo nome, cognome, ecc. [eccɛtera].
Please give me your passport and fill out this registration form with your name, surname, etc.

Vediamo. NOME: John. COGNOME: Brown. CITTA-DINANZA: Stati Uniti d'Amɛrica. . . . Ɛcco fatto.
Let's see. NAME: *John.* SURNAME: *Brown.* CITIZENSHIP: *United States of America. . . . There.*

Benissimo.
Fine.

Mi manda[4] su i bagagli?
Will you send the luggage up?

Li faccio salire[6] subito. Potrà[7] ritirare il passapɔrto quando scende.
I will have it sent up at once. You can get your passport back when you come down.

Grazie.
Thank you.

---

[5] Present subjunctive of **dare**, *to give.* §§ 35, 75 (10).   [6] § 67a.   [7] §75 (21).

(Telefonando) Pronto!
> (*Telephoning*) *Hello!*

Pronto! Cɔsa desidera?
> *Hello! Can I help you (lit. "what do you wish")?*

Per favore mi mandi un altro asciugamano.
> *Please send me another towel.*

Mando subito la cameriɛra, signore.
> *I will send the maid at once, sir.*

(Cameriɛra) È permesso?[8]
> (*Maid*) *May I come in?*

Avanti!
> *Come in!*

Buɔn giorno. Ɛcco gli asciugamani e il sapone.
> *Here are the towels and the soap.*

Puɔ cambiarmi il guanciale? Questo è molto duro.
> *Can you change my pillow? This one is very hard.*

Cɛrto.[9] Desidera più copɛrte? Questi giorni ha fatto[10] piut-
tɔsto freddo.
> *Certainly. Would you like more blankets? It's been (lit.
> "made") rather cold recently (lit. "these days").*

Nɔ, grazie. Ma gradirɛi alcuni attaccapanni. Nell'armadio[11]
ce ne[12] sono soltanto due.
> *No, thank you. But I would like some clothes hangers.
> There are only two in the closet.*

Subito, signore. Se ha bisogno di[13] qualche altra cɔsa, suɔni
il campanɛllo.
> *Right away, sir. If you need anything else, ring the bell.*

Per ora non hɔ bisogno di nulla, grazie.
> *Right now I don't need anything, thank you.*

---

[8] è **permesso**=**permesso?** Also: **si puɔ?**   [9] **cɛrto**=**certamente**=**sicuro.**   [10] § 67.
[11] **armadio a muro,** *wall-closet.*   [12] §§ 33a, 36.   [13] Also: **se Le occorre.**

Vedo che ha finito l'*a*cqua minerale. Ne[12] vuɔle un'altra bott*i*glia?

> *I see that you finished the mineral water. Do you want another bottle?*

Sì, gr*a*zie.

> *Yes, thank you.*

Con gas o sɛnza?[14]

> *Plain or sparkling? (lit. "with gas or without")*

Sɛnza gas, ma non c'è fretta.

> *Plain, but there's no hurry.*

Arrivederla.

> (*Good-bye.*)

Arrivederla.

> (*Good-bye.*)

NƆTE

1. Alternatives when ordering a room: **camera a due lɛtti (matrimoniale)**, *bedroom with twin beds (with a double bed)*.

2. Other expressions of times of day are: **di mattina**, *in the morning*; **di sera**, *in the evening*; **di nɔtte**, *at night*.

3. One may also find **un asciugamano pulito (s*u*dicio**, or **spɔrco)**, *a clean (dirty) towel*; **un asciugamano di spugna**, *a Turkish towel*; **una spa*zz*ola da bagno**, *a bath brush*.

4. An alternative for **guanciale** is **cuscino**. Other useful vocabulary: **fɛdera (di guanciale)**, *pillow case*; **lenzuɔlo** (*pl.* **le lenzuɔla**. § 7*a* (2)), *sheet*.

---

[14] **con gas = gassata; sɛnza gas = l*i*scia.**

La biancheria

The Laundry

(Cameriɛra) Ha suonato?
(Maid) Did you ring?

Sì, signorina. Passi. Ho alcune cɔse da[1] lavare.
Yes (Miss). Come in. I have a few things to be washed.

Quando parte?
When are you leaving?

La settimana prɔssima. Non c'è fretta.
Next week. There's no rush.

Le riporterɔ tutto domani sera.
I'll bring everything back tomorrow evening.

Benissimo. Ɛcco, guardi, ci sono tre cam*i*cie, un pigiama, due fazzoletti, tre p*a*ia[2] di mutandine, tre camiciɔle e tre p*a*ia di calzini.
All right. Look, there are three shirts, a pair of pajamas, two handkerchiefs, three pairs of shorts, three undershirts, and three pairs of socks.

Come preferisce i colletti delle cam*i*cie?
How do you like (lit. "prefer") the collars of your shirts?

Inamidati, ma non trɔppo.
Starched, but not too much.

C'è altro?
Anything else?

[1] § 62b.   [2] **il p*a*io,** *the pair.* § 7a (2).

Sì. Questa giacca è macchiata,[3] guardi.
Yes. This coat has a few spots, look.

La smacchieremo, non si preoccupi.
We'll get it clean, don't worry.

E poi questi pantaloni andrebbero stirati.
And then these pants should be pressed.

Li stirerò io stessa.
I'll press them myself.

Grazie. Buona sera.
Thank you. (Good evening.)

Buona sera. Se vuole farsi lucidare[4] le scarpe le lasci in corridoio.
*(Good evening.) If you want to have your shoes shined,
leave them in the corridor.*

Grazie. (Al telefono) Pronto! Signorina, per favore mi
sveglia[5] alle sette domani mattina?
*Thank you. (Over the telephone) Hello! Will you please
call me (lit. "wake me") tomorrow morning at seven?*

Sì, signore. Buona notte.
Yes, sir. Good night.

Buona notte.
Good night.

NOTE

1. Other useful vocabulary: **calza**, *stocking*; **blusa**, *blouse*;
camicia da notte, *nightgown*; **cravatta**, *necktie*; **gonna**, *skirt*; **abito**,
suit; **vestito**, *dress*.

2. When **andare** is followed by the past participle of a

---

[3] **macchia**, *spot.*   [4] § 67a.   [5] § 45a.

verb, it means "something should be done": **questo va fatto subito,** *this must be done at once*; **l'automobile andrebbe lavata,** *the car should be washed.*

3. Note that, as we do in English, Italians distinguish between *Good evening* (**Buona sera**) and *Good night* (**Buona notte**). **Buona sera**, as you have noticed, is also used with the meaning *Good afternoon* (after around three P.M.).

In giro per Roma

A Tour through Rome

Vuole venire con me a visitare le catacombe di San[1] Callisto?

> *Do you want to come with me to (visit) the catacombs of St. Calixtus?*

Volentieri.   Chiamiamo quel[2] tassì . . . Ci porti all'entrata delle catacombe di San Callisto.

> *Sure (lit. "willingly"). Let's call that taxi. . . . Take us to the entrance of the St. Calixtus catacombs.*

Ieri ho veduto la Basilica di San Paolo e quella di San Giovanni in Laterano.

> *Yesterday I saw St. Paul's and (lit. "the basilica" of St. Paul and that of) St. John Lateran.*

Non ha ancora veduto quella di San Pietro?

> *Haven't you seen St. Peter's yet?*

Ecome! La settimana scorsa. È una chiesa straordinaria.

> *Of course! Last week. It's an extraordinary church.*

Non solo è una chiesa bellissima, ma è la più grande del mondo.

> *Not only is it a very beautiful church, but it's the largest in the world.*

Lo stesso giorno visitai i musei del Vaticano e la Cappella Sistina.

> *The same day I visited the Vatican museums and the Sistine Chapel.*

[1] § 16c.   [2] § 16.

In questo momento passiamo per Piazza Barberini.
Right now we're passing through Barberini Square.

Quella fontana è molto bella. È vero che Roma è piena di belle fontane.
That fountain is very beautiful. Rome is certainly full of lovely fountains.

L'[3] ha già veduto il Colosseo?
Have you seen the Colosseum yet?

Sì. Ci andai con un mio amico che mi fece[4] da[5] guida.
Yes. I went there with a friend of mine who acted as guide.

Io sono sempre vissuto[6] a Roma, ma non la conosco così bene come[7] vorrei.
I've always lived in Rome, but I don't know it as well as I'd like to.

È quasi impossibile vedere tutti i suoi tesori d'arte e i suoi ricordi storici.
It's almost impossible to see all of its art treasures and its historical mementos.

È verissimo. Eccoci arrivati.
That's very true. Here we are.

Quanto segna il tassametro?
How much does the meter say?

Lasci pagare a me.
Let me pay (lit. "leave the paying to me").

No, no, pago io.
No. I'll pay.

Affrettiamoci. [8] Vedo dei turisti che aspettano la guida.[9]
Let's hurry. I see some tourists (who are) waiting for the guide.

---

[3] § 37.   [4] From **fare**. § 75 (15).   [5] § 62*f.*   [6] From **vivere**. § 75 (39).   [7] § 21.
[8] § 35.   [9] **guida** *f.*, *guide* and also *guidebook*.

Davanti a un'ed*i*cola

In front of a Newstand

Ha il giornale del mattino?[1]
> *Do you have the morning paper?*

Sì, signore, l'hanno portato pochi minuti fa.[2]
> *Yes, sir, they brought it a few minutes ago.*

Questo è *Il Messaggεro*, io volevo *Il Tεmpo*.
> *This is* Il Messaggero, *I wanted* Il Tempo.

Il Tεmpo non è ancora arrivato. Dovrεbbe[3] arrivare da un momento all'altro.
> Il Tempo *hasn't arrived yet. It should arrive any minute.*

Ha giornali in l*i*ngua inglese?
> *Do you have any newspapers in English?*

Sì, ho il *Rome Daily American*.
> *Yes, I've got the* Rome Daily American.

Me ne dia[4] uno. Non lo conoscevo.[5]
> *Give me one. I'm not familiar with it (lit "I did not know it").*

Εsce[6] da[7] molti anni. Lo comprano tutti gli Americani che *a*bitano a Roma.
> *It's been coming out for many years. All Americans who live in Rome buy it.*

Ci sono molti Americani a Roma, vero?
> *There are a lot of Americans in Rome, aren't there?*

---

[1] **mattino = mattina.**   [2] § 67c.   [3] §§ 64, 75 (13).   [4] §§ 36c, 75 (10).   [5] § 45b.
[6] From **uscire.** § 75 (36).   [7] § 62a.

Ɛh sì! Diplom*a*tici,[8] u*o*mini[9] di affari, artisti. E p*o*i durante l'estate ci sono molti turisti.

> *Oh . . . yes! Diplomats, businessmen, artists. And then, during the summer there are a lot of tourists.*

Tutti v*o*gliono vi*s*itare la Città Et*e*rna!

> *Everybody wants to visit the Eternal City!*

Ɛcco, signore, hanno portato *Il Tɛmpo* in questo momento.

> *There, sir, they just (lit. "this very minute") brought in* Il Tempo.

Mi dia anche un p*a*io di riviste.

> *Give me a couple of magazines also.*

H*o* *Ɛpoca* e *Oggi*; va bɛne?

> *I've got* Epoca *and* Oggi; *is that all right?*

Ben*i*ssimo. Bu*o*n giorno.

> *Fine. Good-bye.*

Bu*o*n giorno, signore.

> *Good-bye, sir.*

---

[8] § 12.   [9] u*o*mo, *man.*

Il tram e l'*a*utobus

The Streetcar and the Bus

Si ferma qu*i* il tram che va al parco?
> *Does the streetcar that goes to the park stop here?*

Sì, signore. Si ferma proprio qu*i*.
> *Yes, (sir). It stops right here.*

Ogni quanto passa?
> *How often does it come by?*

Ogni diɛci minuti. Sono qua*s*i diɛci minuti che aspɛtto.[1]
> *Every ten minutes. I've been waiting for almost ten minutes.*

Ɛccolo. Ma è piɛno. Tutti i posti sono presi[2] e non c'è posto nemmeno[3] in piedi.
> *Here it is. But it's full. All the seats are taken and there isn't even standing room.*

Non possiamo[4] salire. Ma credo che anche l'*a*utobus si fermi[5] qu*i*.
> *We can't get on. But I believe the bus stops here too.*

Meno male. Domandiamo.[6]
> *That's good. Let's ask.*

Prɛgo,[7] signore, si ferma qu*i* l'*a*utobus che va a Villa Bor-ghese?[8]
> *Excuse me (lit. "I beg"), (sir); does the bus that goes to the Villa Borghese stop here?*

---

[1] *s*ono diɛci minuti che aspɛtto = aspɛtto da diɛci minuti. § 62*a*.   [2] From prɛndere. § 75 (22).   [3] nemmeno = neppure = neanche.   [4] From potere.   § 75 (21).
[5] Present subjunctive of fermarsi. § 48*a*.   [6] Imperative of domandare. § 71.
[7] prɛgo = per favore = per piacere.   [8] A large park in Rome.

Sì, signori. Si ferma proprio qui. Li porterà a due passi[9] dall'entrata.

> *Yes (gentlemen). It stops right here. It'll take you very near the entrance.*

Passa spesso?

> *Does it run often?*

Ogni dieci minuti. Deve venire da un momento all'altro.[10] Io l'aspetto da un quarto d'ora.[1]

> *Every ten minutes. It ought to be coming along any minute now. I've been waiting for it for a quarter of an hour.*

Guardino. Viene in questo momento.

> *Look. It's coming right now.*

Per fortuna non è pieno.

> *Fortunately it's not full.*

Saliamo.

> *Let's get on.*

NOTE

1.   **Prego** is also used with the meaning of *you are welcome* in replying to the word **grazie**, *thank you.*

2.   In the expression **da un momento all' altro**, one may use, for example, **giorno**, *day* to obtain **da un giorno all'altro.**

---

[9] **fare due passi** = **fare una passeggiatina,** *to take a short walk.*   [10] **da un momento all'altro,** *any moment* (lit. "from one moment to the next").

Al musεo

At the Museum

Scusi, dov'è il musεo?
Excuse me, where is the museum?

Ritorni indiεtro fino all'angolo, e vɔlti a sinistra. Quando arriva a Via Mazzini, che è la seconda travεrsa, vedrà il musεo che è dall'altra parte della via.
Go back to the first corner and turn to the left. When you get to Mazzini Street, which is the second crossing, you will see the museum which is across the street.

Grazie mille. (Arrivando) L'entrata è magnіfica. Ma il musεo pare chiuso.
Thank you. (On arriving) The entrance is magnificent. But the museum seems closed.

Desiderava vedere il musεo, signore?
Did you want to see the museum, sir?

Sì. Fino a che ora è apεrto?
Yes. How late is it open?

È già chiuso. Le ore di visita sono dalle trεdici alle sεdici.[1]
It's already closed. Visiting hours are from one to four.

Si paga[2] per entrare, o si entra[2] gratis?
Is there an admission charge, or is it free?

---

[1] **dalle trεdici alle sεdici = dall'una alle quattro (pomeridiane).**   [2] § 59*b* (lit. "does one pay?," "does one go in?").

Le domeniche³ e i giorni festivi⁴ l'entrata è gratis, ma gli altri giorni bisogna pagare.

> *Sundays and holidays there is no admission fee, but on the other days you have to pay.*

La guida si paga² a parte?

> *Is the guide paid separately?*

Sì. C'è una tariffa fissata dallo stato. Ma è bene aggiungere una piccola mancia.

> *Yes. There is a fee which has been set by the State. But it is a good idea to add a small tip.*

C'è un catalogo del museo in vendita?

> *Is there a museum catalogue for sale?*

Sì. Dentro al museo si vendono⁵ cataloghi,⁶ ed anche cartoline illustrate delle opere più importanti.

> *Yes. Catalogues are sold inside the museum, and also post cards with views of the most important works.*

Grazie delle informazioni.

> *Thank you for the information.*

Prego. Venga⁷ presto perchè ci vogliono ⁸ almeno due ore per vedere tutto.

> *You're welcome. Come early because you need at least two hours to see everything.*

NOTE

Other expressions with **giorno**: **giorno feriale** = **giorno di lavoro**, *weekday*; **giorno di riposo**, *day off.*

---

³ § 13.   ⁴ **giorno festivo** *or* **giorno di festa** *m., holiday.*   ⁵ § 59a.   ⁶ **catalogo,** *catalogue.* § 12a.   ⁷ From **venire.** § 75 (38).   ⁸**volere,** *to want,* § 75 (40); **volerci,** *to take* (of time).

Alla banca

At the Bank

Questa è una succursale della Banca Commerciale, non è vero?
This is a branch of the Commercial Bank, isn't it?

Sì, signore. Per servirla.
Yes, sir. What can I do for you? (lit. "to serve you").

Hɔ qui una lɛttera di credito.
I have a letter of credit with me.

Mi vuɔle mostrare il Suo passapɔrto, per favore?
Would you show me your passport, please?

Ɛccolo.
Here it is.

Che somma desidera ritirare?
What amount do you wish to withdraw?

Cɛnto[1] dɔllari. Qual è il cambio?
A hundred dollars. What is the (rate of) exchange?

Ɔggi il cambio non è favorevole per Lɛi.
The exchange is not favorable to you today.

Peccato davvero! Ma hɔ bisogno di denaro.
That's really too bad! But I need money.

Lɛi sa bɛne che il cambio sale[2] e abbassa secondo le ultime notizie politiche e finanziarie.
Of course you know that the rate of exchange rises and falls according to the latest political and financial news.

---

[1] § 76.   [2] **salire,** *to climb, go up, rise.* § 75 (27).

La caduta del governo avrà causato[3] questo ribasso di oggi.
> *The fall of the government must have caused today's fall.*

È proprio così. (Contando) Dieci, venti, trenta, quaranta, cinquanta, sessanta, settanta, ottanta, novanta, cento.
> *That's right. (Counting) Ten, twenty, thirty, forty, fifty, sixty, seventy, eighty, ninety, a hundred.*

Vorrei[4] anche cambiare quest'assegno.
> *I should also like to cash this check.*

Vuole firmarlo, per favore?
> *Will you endorse it, please?*

Ecco fatto. Domani verrà[5] un mio amico ad aprire un conto. Vuole depositare mille dollari.
> *There (lit. "behold it done"). A friend of mine is coming here tomorrow to open an account. He wants to deposit one thousand dollars.*

Benissimo. Qui si dà il tre per cento.
> *Fine. We pay three percent here.*

Non è molto.
> *That's not much.*

No, ma come dice[6] il proverbio "è meglio un uovo oggi che una gallina domani."
> *No, but as the saying goes "a bird in the hand is worth two in the bush" (lit. "an egg today is better than a hen tomorrow").*

NOTE

1. **Banco** is also used for **banca**.

2. **Assegno** also suggests: **firmare un assegno (uno cheque),**

---

[3] **avrà causato**, future perfect of conjecture = **probabilmente ha causato**. § 45*d*.
[4] From **volere**. § 75 (40).   [5] From **venire**. § 75 (38).   [6] § 75 (11).

to sign a check; **falsificare,** *to forge*; **libretto di assegni bancari** *m.,* *checkbook*; **assegno turistico** or **assegno per viaggiatori,** *traveler's check.*

3. Other useful vocabulary: **fare un deposito,** *to make a deposit*; **depositante** *m.* and *f., depositor*; **cassa di risparmio,** *savings bank*; **libretto (della cassa di risparmio)** *m., bankbook, passbook*; **conto corrente** *m., checking account.*

Giorni festivi

Holidays

(Al portiɛre dell'albɛrgo) Sono andato all'ufficio postale[1] ma ɛra chiuso. Perchè? Ɔggi non è domenica.

> *(To the concierge at the hotel) I went to the post office but it was closed. Why? Today isn't Sunday.*

Perchè ɔggi è il due giugno ed è fɛsta nazionale, signore.

> *Because today is June 2 and it's a national holiday (sir).*

Corrisponde forse alla fɛsta del quattro luglio negli Stati Uniti?

> *Does it correspond in some way (lit. "perhaps") to the Fourth of July holiday in the United States?*

In un cɛrto sɛnso. Il due giugno 1946 (mille novecɛnto quarantasɛi)[2] fu fondata la Repubblica Italiana.

> *In a way. On June 2, 1946, the Italian Republic was founded.*

È una repubblica molto giovane.

> *It's a very young Republic.*

È vero. Infatti la Costituzione Italiana entrɔ in vigore il primo [3] gennaio 1948 (mille novecɛnto quarantɔtto).

> *Right. In fact the Italian Constitution became effective on January 1, 1948.*

Avete molte fɛste in Italia, vero?[4]

> *You have a lot of holidays in Italy, haven't you?*

---

[1] **ufficio postale** = **pɔsta** *f.*   [2] § 76.   [3] § 77.   [4] **vero?** = **non è vero?** *is it not so?*

Anche trɔppe! Fɛste civili e fɛste religiose.

Too many! Civic holidays and religious holidays.

Le vɔstre grandi fɛste religiose come il Natale e la Pasqua, perɔ, corrispɔndono alle nɔstre.

Your main religious holidays such as Christmas and Easter, however, are the same as (lit. "correspond to") ours.

Naturalmente. Ma vi sono delle differɛnze. Per esɛmpio qua in Italia è fɛsta il giorno dopo Natale, il lunedì dopo Pasqua, il giorno di San Giusɛppe (il diciannɔve marzo) e il giorno dell'Assunzione della Beata Vergine (il quindici agosto).

Naturally. But there are some differences. For example, here in Italy the day after Christmas, the Monday after Easter, St. Joseph's Day (March 19) and the day of the Assumption of the Blessed Virgin (August 15) are holidays.

Il quindici agosto è anche Ferragosto, vero?[4]

August 15 is also called Ferragosto, isn't it?

Sì. Lɛi è stato mai in Italia il giorno di Ferragosto?

Yes. Have you ever been in Italy on Ferragosto?

Sì, tre anni fa. Ricɔrdo che hɔ attraversato mɛzza città a piɛdi sɛnza cɔrrere il perɪcolo d'ɛssere investito da una macchina!

Yes, three years ago. I remember that I crossed half the city on foot without having to worry about (lit. "running the danger of") being run over by a car.

Non mi sorprɛnde; quasi tutti i Romani ɛrano fuɔri città!

That's not surprising; nearly all the Romans were out of town.

NOTE

1. **I mesi dell'anno sono** (*the months of the year are*): **gennaio** (*January*), **febbraio** (*February*), **marzo** (*March*), **aprile**

(*April*), **maggio** (*May*), **giugno** (*June*), **luglio** (*July*), **agosto** (*August*), **settembre** (*September*), **ottobre** (*October*), **novembre** (*November*), **dicembre** (*December*).

    2.   *Is it true?* is translated by è **vero?** or **davvero?**

    3.   As in **senza correre**, after a preposition the English gerund is translated by the infinitive, e.g., **prima di partire**, *before leaving*.

Il telɛfono

The Telephone

Scusi, cerco un elɛnco telefɔnico della città.
Excuse me, I'm looking for a telephone directory of the city.

Guardi, signore, ce n'ɛ uno[1] nella cabina telefɔnica.
Look, sir, there's one in the telephone booth.

Grazie ... Ɛccolo, Balɛstra Egidio: 51–63–17 (cinquantuno-sessantatrɛ-diciassɛtte).
Thanks. . . . Here it is, Balestra Egidio: 51-63-17.

Pronto? Signorina, mi dà[2] per favore questo numero ... ?
Hello? Operator, would you please get me this number..?

Signore, puɔ formare il numero Lɛi stesso.
You can dial the number yourself, sir.

Ah, sì, ɛ vero.
Oh, yes, of course (lit. "it's true").

(Forma il numero) Pronto? Ɛ il Signor Moretti Lɛi?
(Dials the number) Hello? (Is this) Mr. Moretti?

Sì. Con chi parlo?
Yes. Who is this speaking?

Io sono Robert Martin.
This is Robert Martin.

Robɛrto chi?
Robert who?

[1] §§ 36, 38.   [2] § 45a.

Martin! Milano, Arezzo, Roma, Torino, *I*mola, Napoli.
> *Martin! M as in Milan, A as in Arezzo, R as in Rome, T as in Turin, I as in Imola, N as in Naples.*

Ah, come va? Aspettavo la Sua telefonata.
> *Well! How are you? I was expecting your call.*

Come? Non sɛnto. Pronto!
> *What? I can't hear. Hello!*

Aspettavo la Sua telefonata da un momento all'altro.
> *I was expecting your call any minute.*

Parli più fɔrte, per favore.
> *Speak louder, please.*

Aspettavo la Sua telefonata . . .
> *I was expecting your call. . .*

Si avvicini al micrɔfono.
> *Get closer to the mouthpiece (lit. "microphone").*

Aspettavo la Sua . . .
> *I was expecting your. . .*

Sono in una cabina e c'è molto rumore. Non sɛnto niɛnte.[3]
> *I'm in a telephone booth and there's a lot of noise. I can't hear a thing.*

Passerɔ dal[4] Suo albɛrgo.
> *I'll come by your hotel.*

Viɛne al mio albɛrgo?
> *Are you coming to my hotel?*

Sì, perchè non sɛnto niɛnte.
> *Yes, because I can't hear a thing.*

Nemmeno io. L'aspetterɔ all'albɛrgo.
> *Neither can I. I'll wait for you at the hotel.*

[3] § 32*b*.   [4] § 62*e*.

A più tardi.
See you later.

NOTE

In spelling out names over the telephone in Italy the initials of well-known cities are used.

Macchine fotografiche e accessori

Cameras and Photographic Supplies

Desidero fare stampare queste fotografie.
I'd like to have these pictures printed.

Sì, signore. Se le lascia ora, saranno pronte domani sera alle sei.
Yes, sir. If you leave them now, they'll be ready tomorrow evening at six.

Va bene. Lascio questi tre rollini. Desidero due copie di ogni fotografia.
All right. I'll leave these three rolls. I want two prints of each (picture).

Ha bisogno di film?
Do you need any film?

Sì, mi dia[1] due rollini da venti fotografie.
Yes, give me two rolls of twenty exposures.

Di che numero?
What number?

Per questa macchina da 35 (trentacinque) millimetri. Saprebbe dirmi perchè riuscirono così male queste foto che feci[2] la settimana scorsa?
For this 35-millimeter camera. Could you tell me why these pictures that I took last week turned out so badly?

---

[1] From **dare**. § 75 (10).   [2] From **fare**. § 75 (15).

Vediamo. Questa non fu esposta sufficientemente, e questa è sfocata.[3]

> *Let's see. This one was underexposed, and this one is not in focus.*

E queste?

> *And these?*

Queste hanno preso[4] trɔppa luce. Evidentemente la Sua macchina non funziona bɛne.

> *These are overexposed (lit. "have taken too much light").*
> *Evidently, something is wrong with your camera (lit. "does not function well").*

La puɔ accomodare?

> *Can you repair it?*

Sì, ma dovrà lasciarla qu*i* per una settimana perchè abbiamo molto lavoro.

> *Yes, but you'll have to leave it here for a week, because we're very busy.*

Va bɛne. Non hɔ fretta. Sɛnta, vorrɛi un paio d'occhiali da sole.

> *All right. I'm not in a hurry. Say (lit. "listen"), I'd like a pair of sun glasses.*

Le piacciono questi con la montatura di tartaruga?

> *Do you like these with the tortoise-shell frame?*

Perfɛtti. Li prɛndo.

> *Perfect. I'll take them.*

Grazie. Buɔn giorno.

> *Thank you. (Good-bye.)*

Buɔn giorno.

> *(Good-bye.)*

---

[3] **sfocata** = **fuɔri fuɔco**, *out of focus*; **mettere a fuɔco**, *to focus*.   [4] From **prɛndere**. § 75 (22).

NOTE

1. **macchina fotografica** = **apparecchio fotografico**. Other vocabulary: **macchina cinematografica**, *movie camera*; **camera oscura**, *darkroom*; **fotografo**, *photographer*; **dilettante** *m.* and *f.*, *amateur*.

2. **accessori** *m. pl.* = *materials, supplies*. Other vocabulary: **esposimetro** *exposure meter*; **filtro**, *filter*; **fissativo** or **bagno di fissaggio**, *fixative*; **lastra**, *plate*; **otturatore** *m.*, *shutter*; **rivelatore** *m.* or **bagno di sviluppo**, *developer*; **telemetro**, *range finder*; (tele-) **obiettivo**, (*telescopic*) *lens*; **treppiede** *m.* (**cavalletto**), *tripod*

3. **rollino** = **rotolo**, *roll of film*; **a colori** (**in bianconero**), *color* (*black and white*) *picture*; **diapositiva**, *slide*; **pellicola di sedici millimetri**, *sixteen-millimeter film*; **lampadina lampo** *f.*, *flashbulb*.

4. **foto** = **fotografia**. Other vocabulary: **istantanea**, *snapshot*; **posa**, *time exposure*; **prova**, *proof*; **negativa**, *negative*; **positiva**, *positive*; **ingrandimento**, *enlargement*; **stampare**, *to print*.

5. **fare** (**prendere**) **un'istantanea** (**una fotografia**), *to take a picture*; **ritrattarsi**, *to have one's picture taken*; **montare**, *to mount*; **ritoccare**, *to retouch*; **mi sono ritrattato** (**fotografato**) **ieri**, *I had my picture taken yesterday*.

Al ristorante

At the Restaurant

■ **La colazione**   *Breakfast*

Sɛrvono la colazione quⁱ?
> *Is breakfast served here?*

Sì, signore. Si accɔmodi quⁱ.
> *Yes, sir. Sit down here.*

Mi pɔrti un bicchiɛre di succo d'arancio, due uɔva[1] e pane tostato.
> *Bring me a glass of orange juice, two eggs, and toast.*

Come desⁱdera le uɔva: alla cɔque, fritte o strapazzate?
> *How do you want the eggs: soft-boiled, fried, or scrambled?*

Fritte con prosciutto cɔtto.
> *Fried with ham.*

Mi dispiace, ma non abbiamo prosciutto cɔtto.
> *I'm sorry, but we have no ham.*

Allora strapazzate con formaggio.
> *In that case scrambled with cheese.*

Benⁱssimo. E cɔsa vuɔle bere: caffè, cioccolata o tè?
> *Very well. And what do you want to drink: coffee, chocolate, or tea?*

Caffè e latte.
> *Coffee and milk.*

---

[1] **uɔvo** *m. egg* (*pl.* **le uɔva**). § 7a (2).

Benissimo.
> *Fine.*

Non ha tardato molto, ma ha dimenticato lo zucchero e il burro.
> *It didn't take you long, but you've forgotten the sugar and the butter.*

Torno [2] subito. Ecco tutto.
> *I'll be right back. Here's everything.*

Grazie. (Più tardi) Il conto, per favore.
> *Thank you. (Later) The check, please.*

Eccolo. Tante grazie.
> *Here it is. Thank you.*

Il servizio è compreso?
> *Is service included?*

Sì, signore.
> *Yes, sir.*

■ **Il pranzo**   *Dinner*

Entriamo in questo ristorante.
> *Let's go into this restaurant.*

Ho sentito dire che qui si mangia bene.
> *I've heard (say) that the food is good here.*

Sediamoci a questo tavolo d'angolo.
> *Let's sit down at this corner table.*

Io ho una fame da[3] lupi.
> *I'm as hungry as a bear (lit. "wolf").*

Ecco il cameriere. (Al cameriere) Ci porti la lista.
> *Here's the waiter. (To the waiter) Bring us the menu.*

---

[2] **tornare = ritornare; torno subito = vado e (ri)torno.**   [3] § 62c.

Ɛccola. Abbiamo anche il pranzo a prɛzzo fisso. Il piatto del giorno è pollo arrɔsto.

> *Here it is. We have also a regular dinner (lit. "at a set price"). Today's specialty is roast chicken.*

Vogliamo cominciare con la minɛstra.

> *We want to begin with the soup.*

Abbiamo minɛstra di taglierini e passato di pisɛlli.

> *We have noodle soup and thick pea soup.*

Ci pɔrti due minɛstre di taglierini.

> *Bring us two noodle soups.*

Benissimo. E che altro?

> *Very well. And what else?*

Io prɛndo il pollo e un'insalata verde.

> *I'll take the chicken and a green salad.*

E io una bistecca ai fɛrri bɛn cɔtta con patate fritte.

> *And I'll have a broiled (or grilled) steak, well done, with fried potatoes.*

Ci pɔrti anche acqua minerale e un fiaschetto[4] di Chianti.

> *Also bring us mineral water and a small bottle of Chianti.*

E che frutta[5] desiderano?

> *And what fruit would you like?*

Non impɔrta, purchè sia[6] fresca.

> *It doesn't matter, provided it's fresh.*

(Più tardi) Ma queste pere sono un pɔ' guaste.[7]

> *(Later) But these pears are a little spoiled.*

Allora affrettiamoci[8] a mangiarle[9] prima che vadano[10] completamente a male.

> *Then let's hurry up and eat them before they spoil completely.*

---

[4] **fiasco,** *flask*. § 17*b*.   [5] **frutta** (*pl.* **frutta** and **frutte**), *fruit* (for eating).
[6] Present subjunctive of **ɛssere**. §§ 75 (14), 50*d*.   [7] **guastarsi** = **andare a male**, *to spoil* (fruit).   [8] § 35.   [9] § 34.   [10] Present subjunctive of **andare**. §§ 75 (1), 50*b*.

(Cameriɛre) Prɛndono caffɛ̀?
(Waiter) Will you have coffee?

Nɔ. Il conto, per favore.
No. The check, please.

NOTE

1.   Many people use **prima colazione** for *breakfast* and **colazione** for *lunch*.

2.   Other vocabulary suggested by **caffɛ̀, tɛ̀**, etc.: **caffettiɛra**, *coffeepot*; **cioccolatiɛra**, *chocolate pot*; **teiɛra**, *teapot*.

3.   In Italy it is customary to put milk in one's coffee rather than *cream* (**panna**). The spelling **caffɛlatte** (*m.*) is also found.

4.   **pranzo** is used for *meal* in general and specifically *dinner*. In many parts of Italy the heavy meal is served at noon (especially on Sundays and holidays) and is called **il pranzo**; the lighter evening meal is then **la cena** (six to eight P.M.). Elsewhere the noontime meal may be called **la colazione** (*lunch*) and the early evening meal is **il pranzo** (*dinner*).

5.   The opposite of **bɛn cɔtta** is **al sangue**, *rare* or *medium rare* (lit. "bloody").

6.   Restaurants may also have a wine list (**lista dei vini**).

7.   Other useful vocabulary: **passare**, *to become tainted* (meat); **questa carne ɛ̀ passata**, *this meat is tainted* (or *spoiled*).

Cibi e bevande

Food and Drinks

■ Condimenti *Seasonings*

aceto *m.* vinegar
aglio *m.* garlic
burro *m.* butter
cannɛlla *f.* cinnamon
capperi *m. pl.* capers
fungo *m.* mushroom
maionese *f.* mayonnaise
mostarda *or* sɛnape *f.* mustard

noce moscata *f.* nutmeg
ɔlio *m.* oil
pepe *m.* pepper
sale *m.* salt
salsa di pomodɔro *f.* catchup
spɛzie *f. pl.* spices
zucchero *m.* sugar

■ Pane *Bread*

crɔsta *f.* crust; midolla *or*
  mollica *f.* soft part
fetta *f.* slice
grissino *m.* bread stick
pane bianco *m.* white bread
pane di granturco *m.* corn bread
pane di sɛgale *m.* rye bread

pane duro *or* stantio *m.* stale
  bread
pane fatto in casa *or* casalingo
  m. homemade bread
pane fresco *m.* fresh bread
pane nero *m.* dark bread
panino *m.* roll

■ Antipasti *Hors D'Œuvres*

acciuga *f.* anchovy
carciofino *m.* little artichoke

cetriuɔlo sotto aceto *m.* pickled
  cucumber

cipolla *f.* onion
cipollina *f.* green onion
finocchio *m.* fennel
oliva *f.* olive
prosciutto *m.* Italian ham
ravanello *m.* radish

salame *m.* salame
salsiccia *f.* sausage
sardina *f.* sardine
sedano *m.* celery
tonno *m.* tuna

■ Minestre   *Soups*

brodo *m.* broth
brodo ristretto *m.* consommé
fettuccine al burro *f. pl.* noodles
with butter
minestra di cipolla *f.*   onion
soup
minestra di fagiuoli *f.*   bean
soup
minestra di lenticchie *f.* lentil
soup
minestra di pollo *f.*   chicken
soup
minestra di riso *f.*   rice soup

minestra di taglierini *f.*   noodle
soup
minestrone *m.*   thick vegetable
soup
passato di piselli *m.*   thick pea
soup
risotto alla milanese *m.*   rice
Milanese style
spaghetti al sugo (al burro) *m.*
pl. spaghetti with sauce (with
butter)
zuppa di cavolo *f.* cabbage soup
zuppa di ceci *f.* chick-pea soup

■ Uova   *Eggs*

albume *m. or* chiara *f. or* bianco
d'uovo *m.* egg white
frittata *f.* omelette
frittata di carciofi *f.* artichoke
omelette
torlo *or* rosso d'uovo *m.* yolk
uova alla coque *f. pl.* soft-boiled
eggs
uova in camicia *f. pl.* poached
eggs

uova fresche *f. pl.* fresh eggs
uova fritte *f. pl.* fried eggs
uova ripiene *f. pl.* stuffed eggs
uova sode *f. pl.* hard-boiled
eggs
uova strapazzate *f. pl.* scram-
bled eggs
uovo *m.* egg

■ Pesci e frutti di mare   *Sea Food*

anguilla *f.* eel
aragosta *f.* lobster
aringa (affumicata) *f.* (smoked) herring
baccalà *m.* stockfish
calamaro *m.* or seppia *f.* squid
cɔzze *f. pl.* mussels
gamberetto di mare *m.* shrimp
gambero d'acqua dolce *m.* crayfish
granchio *m.* crab

merluzzo *m.* cod
ɔstrica *f.* oyster
pesce marinato *m.* marinated fish
salmone *m.* salmon
scampi (fritti) *m. pl.* (fried) shrimp
sɔgliola *f.* sole
triglia *f.* mullet
trɔta *f.* trout

■ Carne   *Meat*

agnɛllo *m.* lamb
animɛlle *f. pl.* sweetbreads
bistecca *f.* beefsteak
capretto *m.* kid
cervɛllo *m.* brain
coniglio *m.* rabbit
cɔscia d'agnɛllo *f.* leg of lamb
costoletta *or* braciɔla *f.* chop, cutlet
fegato *m.* liver
filetto *m.* filet, tenderloin
lingua *f.* tongue

maiale (arrɔsto) *m.* (roast) pork
manzo *or* bue *m.* beef
montone *m.* mutton
polpetta *f.* meat ball
rognoni *m. pl.* kidneys
rosbif *m.* roast beef
salsiccia *f.* sausage
scaloppine *f. pl.* small veal cutlets
stufato *m.* stew
trippa *f.* tripe
vitɛllo *m.* veal

■ Pollame   *Fowl*

anitra *f.* duck
cappone *m.* capon
gallina *f.* hen
ɔca *f.* goose

pɛtto di pollo *m.* breast of chicken
pollo (arrɔsto) *m.* (roast) chicken

pollo ai ferri *m.* broiled chicken
pollo lesso *m.* boiled chicken
tacchino arrosto *m.* roast turkey

tacchino ripieno *m.* stuffed turkey

■ Selvaggina *Game*

anitra selvatica *f.* wild duck
beccaccia *f.* woodcock
cervo *m.* deer
cinghiale *m.* wild boar

fagiano *m.* pheasant
lepre *f.* Belgian hare
pernice *f.* partridge
quaglia *f.* quail

■ Verdure *Vegetables*

aglio *m.* garlic
asparago *m.* asparagus
barbabietola *f.* beet
broccoli *m. pl.* broccoli
carciofo *m.* artichoke
carota *f.* carrot
cavolfiore *m.* cauliflower
cavolo *m.* cabbage
ceci *m. pl.* chick-peas
cetriuolo *m.* cucumber
cicoria *f.* chicory
cipolla *f.* onion
crescione *m.* water cress
fagiolini *m. pl.* string beans
fagiuoli *m. pl.* beans
funghi *m. pl.* mushrooms
granturco *m.* corn

indivia *f.* endive
lattuga *f.* lettuce
melanzana *f.* eggplant
passato *or* purè di patate *m.* mashed potatoes
patata (fritta, bollita) *f.* (*fried,* boiled) potato
peperone *m.* pepper
piselli *m. pl.* peas
pomodoro (ripieno) *m.* (stuffed) tomato
prezzemolo *m.* parsley
rapa *f.* turnip
ravanello *m.* radish
spinaci *m. pl.* spinach
zucchini *m. pl.* Italian squash

■ Dolci *Sweets, Desserts*

biscotto *m.* cookie
crema *f.* custard

gelato *m.* ice cream
marmellata *f.* marmalade

meringa *f.* meringue
miɛle *m.* honey
millefɔglie *m.* a very light multi-
  layered custard cake
pasta *f.* pastry, cookie
sorbetto *m.* sherbet

spumone *m.* spumone ice cream
torta *f.* cake
ʒabaione *m.* a dessert made
  with yolks of eggs, Marsala
  wine and sugar

■ **Frutta e formaggi**   *Fruit and Cheeses*

albicɔcca *f.* apricot
ananas *m.* pineapple
arancia *f.* orange
banana *f.* banana
Bɛl Paese *m.* Bel Paese cheese
ciliɛgia *f.* cherry
cocomero *m.* watermelon
dattero *m.* date
fico d'India *m.* prickly pear
fico (secco) *m.* (dry) fig
fragola *f.* strawberry
gorgonʒola *f.* Gorgonzola
  cheese
groviɛra *f.* Swiss cheese
lampone *m.* raspberry
limone *m.* lemon
mandarino *m.* tangerine
mandorla *f.* almond
mela *f.* apple
melacotɔgna *f.* quince

mela cɔtta (cruda), baked (raw)
  apple
melagrana *f.* pomegranate
mirtillo *m.* blueberry
mɔra *f.* blackberry
nocciɔla *f.* hazelnut
nɔcciolo *m.* stone
noce *f.* walnut
parmigiano *m.* Parmesan cheese
pera *f.* pear
pompelmo *m.* grapefruit
popone *m.* (*or* **melone** *m.*)
  melon
provolone *m.* Provolone cheese
ribes *m.* currant
seme *m.* seed
susina *f.* plum
uva *f.* grape(s)
uva passa *or* **uva secca** *f.* raisins
uva spina *f.* gooseberry

■ **Bevande**   *Drinks*

acqua (potabile) *f.* (drinking)
  water
acqua di Sɛltz *f.* soda water

acqua minerale *f.* mineral
  water (**gassata,** sparkling;
  liscia, plain)

*a*lcool *m.* alcohol
aperitivo *m.* apéritif
aranciata *f.* orangeade
b*i*bita *f.* soft drink
birra *f.* beer
cacao *m.* cocoa
caffè *m.* coffee
cappuccino *m.* esprɛsso coffee
with milk
cognac *m.* brandy
esprɛsso *m.* a strong coffee pre-
pared by forcing live steam
under   pressure   through
ground   dark-roast   coffee
beans
latte *m.* milk
latte pastorizzato *m.* pasteur-
ized milk
limonata *f.* lemonade
liquore *m.* liqueur

Marsala *m.* a sherry-type wine
pɔnce *m.* punch
rum *m.* rum
sciampagna *f.* champagne
sidro *m.* cider
tè *m.* tea
vino *m.* wine
vino asciutto (or secco) *m.* dry
wine
vino bianco *m.* white wine
vino da t*a*vola *or* da pasto *m.*
table wine
vino dolce *m.* sweet wine
vino leggiɛro (fɔrte *or* generoso)
m. light (strong) wine
vino moscato *m.* muscatel
vino rosso *m.* red wine
vino spumante *m.* sparkling
wine

■ La tavola   *The Table*

bicchiɛre *m.* glass
bott*i*glia *f.* bottle
coltɛllo *m.* knife
cucchiaino *m.* teaspoon
cucchi*a*io *m.* spoon
forchetta *f.* fork
piatto *m.* dish, plate

piattino *m.* saucer
sɛdia *f.* chair
tazza *f.* cup
tazzina *f.* demi-tasse
tov*a*glia *f.* tablecloth
tovagliɔlo *m.* napkin

3

In giro per l'Italia

Traveling Around Italy

Autonoleggio

Car Rental

Buɔn giorno.
> *Good morning.*

Buɔn giorno. Ill signore des*i*dera?
> *Good morning. What can I do for you?*

Vorrɛi[1] noleggiare una macchina.[2]
> *I would like to rent a car.*

Vuɔle una macchina p*i*ccola, mɛdia o grande?
> *Do you want a small, medium, or large car?*

Una macchina mɛdia a due sportɛlli.
> *A medium, two-door car.*

Per quanto tɛmpo?
> *For how long (lit. "for how much time")?*

Per una settimana.
> *A week.*

La riporterà qu*i* o des*i*dera restituirla in un'altra città?
> *Will you be bringing it back here or do you want to return it in another city?*

La restituirɔ all'agenzia di N*a*poli.
> *I'll turn it in at the Naples agency.*

Ha la patɛnte di guida?
> *Do you have a driver's license?*

---

[1] From **volere**, *to want*. § 75 (40).   [2] **macchina** = **autom**ɔ**bile** = **vettura**.

Sì. Hɔ la patɛnte internazionale.
> *Yes. I have an international driver's license.*

Vuɔle mostrɑrmela?
> *May I see it (lit. "do you want to show it to me")?*

Ɛccola.
> *Here it is.*

E ora firmi questo contratto.
> *And now sign this contract.*

Mi dà per favore una pianta della città e una carta stradale dell'Itɑlia centrale?
> *Would you please give me a map of the city and a road map of central Italy?*

Ɛccole. Ed ɛcco le chiavi della mɑcchina.
> *Here they are. And here are the car keys.*

Dov'ɛ la mɑcchina?
> *Where is the car?*

Quɪ fuɔri. Ɛ davanti alla pɔrta. Vɛnga,[3] gliela[4] ɪndico io.
> *Right outside. It's in front of the door. Come this way; I'll show it to you.*

Ah! Dimenticavo. Ɛ assicurata?
> *Oh! I was forgetting. Is it insured?*

Sì, sì. Non si preɔccupi.
> *Yes, of course. Don't worry.*

NɔTE

1. If a *four-door* model is needed, one asks for a car **a quattro sportɛlli**.

2. Other regions of Italy: **Itɑlia settentrionale** or **del nɔrd**, *northern Italy*; **Itɑlia meridionale** or **del sud**, *southern Italy*.

---

[3] From **venire**, *to come* § 75 (38).   [4] § 36.

Il viaggio in automobile

The Automobile Trip

■ **La partenza**   *Setting off*

Scusi. C'è una stazione di servizio[1] qui vicino?
> *Excuse me. Is there a service station near here?*

Sì, signore; dietro all'angolo.
> *Yes (sir); around the corner.*

Grazie. . . . Ah, eccola.
> *Thank you . . . oh, there it is.*

Buon giorno. Desidera benzina?
> *Hi. Do you want some gasoline?*

Sì. Faccia[2] il pieno.
> *Yes. Fill up the tank.*

Ecco fatto. Venticinque litri.[3]
> *There you are. Twenty-five liters.*

Vuole controllare la pressione delle gomme, per favore?
> *Would you check the air in the tires please?*

Volentieri. Tutto è a posto. Ho controllato anche l'olio e l'acqua. Se vuole, Le lavo il parabrezza che è sporco.
> *Glad to. Everything's all right. I checked the oil and the water, too. If you want, I'll wash the windshield; it is dirty.*

---

[1] **stazione di servizio** *f.* = **stazione di rifornimento** *f.*   [2] **faccia** is subjunctive of **fare**. § 75 (15).   [3] § 78.

Sì, grazie.
> *Yes, thank you.*

Sa se questa è la strada che va a Napoli?
> *Do you know if this is the road that goes to Naples?*

Sì, ma è lunga. Le merita conto prendere l'autostrada.
> *Yes, but it's (the) long (way). It would be worth your while to take the freeway.*

Dov'è l'autostrada?
> *Where's the freeway?*

Vada[4] diritto fino al secondo semaforo e poi volti a destra. Non può sbagliare.
> *Go straight ahead to the second light and then turn right. You can't miss.*

Grazie.
> *Thank you.*

Buon viaggio.
> *Have a good trip.*

NOTE

Other useful vocabulary: **pompa della benzina = distributore di benzina** *m.*, *gasoline pump*; **inserviente** *m.* or *f.*, *attendant*; **serbatoio**, *tank*; **tergicristallo** *windshield wiper*; **strada di uscita**, *off ramp*; **strada di entrata**, *on ramp*; **strada (a due carreggiate)**, *(two-lane) highway*.

---

[4] From **andare**, *to go* § 75 (1).

In viaggio

On the Road

È questa la strada più corta per andare a Sorrɛnto?
Is this the shortest road (to go) to Sorrento?

Nɔ, signore, ma è la più bɛlla.
No (sir), but it's the most beautiful.

È in buɔno stato?
Is it in good condition?

Sì; è tutta asfaltata.

Yes, it's all paved.

Sa[1] se vi sono deviazioni?
Do you know whether there are any detours?

Nɔ. Ci sono però alcune curve pericolose.
No. But there are some dangerous curves.

Farò attenzione. E pɔi, i frɛni di questa mɑcchina funzionano bɛne.
I'll be careful. And anyhow, the brakes on this car are working well.

Se è così, può star tranquillo.
If that's so, you needn't worry.

Li hɔ fatti[2] aggiustare perchè vɔglio andare anche ad Amalfi.
I had them adjusted because I want to go to Amalfi also.

---

[1] **sapere**, *to know* (a thing). § 75 (28).   [2] §§ 67a, 43a.

Ha fatto bɛne, perchè in quella strada ci sono molte curve.

>   *I don't blame you (lit. "you did well"); (because) there are a lot of curves on that road.*

Per sicurezza suonerɔ il clacson in tutte le curve.

>   *To be on the safe side (lit. "for safety"), I'll blow the horn on all the curves.*

Buɔn viaggio.

>   *Have a nice trip.*

NɔTE

1.   Other vocabulary: **crocevia** *m.*, or **incrocio**, *crossroads*; **passaggio a livɛllo**, railroad crossing.

2.   **ad** and **ed** are frequently used instead of **a**, *to*, *at*, *in*, and **e**, *and*, before a word which begins with a vowel.

Il garage

The Garage

C'è un'officina di riparazioni qu*i* vicino?
Is there a repair shop around here?

Sì, è in qu*e*l garage di fronte.
Yes, in that garage across the way (or *directly opposite*).

Gr*a*zie. . . .
Thank you. . . .

Bu*ɔ*n giorno. La Sua m*a*cchina non funziona b*ɛ*ne?
Good morning. Something wrong with your car?

N*ɔ*. Le candele sono sp*ɔ*rche.
Yes. The spark plugs need cleaning (lit. "are dirty").

Ha notato altro?
Have you noticed anything else?

Sì. Il radiatore v*ɛ*rsa, e il motore d*ɛ*tona e riscalda in salita.
Yes. The radiator leaks, and the motor knocks and heats too much going uphill.

Vediamo. . . . A quanto pare l'accumulatore[1] non c*a*rica. Dovr*ɔ* riguardarlo.
Let's see. . . . *Seems the battery isn't charging. I'll have to check it.*

Quanto ci vu*ɔ*le[2] a far tutto?
How long will it take to do all that?

---

[1] Also: **batteria.**   [2] **volere**, *to want*, § 75 (40); **volerci** *to take* (of time).

Circa due ore. Quando finirò,[3] Le darò un colpo di telɛfono.
About two hours. I'll phone you when I finish.

Sta bɛne. Io sarò all'albɛrgo. Dɛvo[4] chiudere l'automɔbile a chiave?[5]
All right. I'll be at the hotel. Do I have to lock the car?

Non ɛ necessɑrio. Però mi lasci le chiavi.
No need. But leave the keys with me.

Ɛccole. Quanto costeranno le riparazioni?
Here they are. How much will the repairs cost?

Non lo sɔ ancora. Ma i nɔstri prɛzzi sono mɔdici.
I don't know yet. But our prices are reasonable (lit. "moderate").

NƆTE

1. Some alternative vocabulary: **rotto (-a)**, *out of order, broken*; **in discesa**, *downhill*; **in pianura**, *on a level road.*

2. Additional vocabulary: **allentare**, *to loosen*; **ammortizzatore** *m.*, *shock absorber*; **fermarsi (il motore)**, *to stop, stall*; **gonfiare**, *to inflate*; **ingrassare, (lubrificare)**, *to grease (lubricate)*; **mɔlla**, *spring*; **non si apre**, *doesn't open*; **non si chiude**, *doesn't close*; **pulire il carburatore**, *to clean the carburetor*; **sgonfiare**, *to deflate*; **silenziatore** *m.*, *muffler*; **smerigliare le vɑlvole**, *to grind the valves*; **stringere**, *to tighten*; **un corto circuito**, *a short circuit*; **ventilatore** *m.*, *fan*; **verniciare**, *to paint.*

3. Other vocabulary suggested by **prɛzzi**: **i prɛzzi sono alti (salati)**, *the prices are high (sky-high)*; **a buɔn mercato**, *cheap.*

---

[3] § 45*f* [4] **dovere**, *to have to, must*. §§ 65*b*, 75 (13). [5] **chiudere**, *to close*; **chiave** *f. key.*

Il viaggio in piroscafo

The Trip by Ship

■ **All'agenzia di navigazione**   *At the Steamship Agency*

Quando parte il prɔssimo pirɔscafo per Palɛrmo?
When does the next ship for Palermo sail?

Il *Vulcano* parte domani sera.
The Vulcan *sails tomorrow evening.*

A che ora?
(At) what time?

Parte alle venti e arriva la mattina dopo alle nɔve.
It sails at 8:00 P.M., and it arrives the following morning at nine.

Vorrɛi[1] riservare[2] una cabina di seconda classe.
I would like to reserve a second-class cabin.

Benissimo, la cabina numero quindici ɛ disponibile.
Fine; cabin number 15 is available.

La traversata ɛ dirɛtta a Palɛrmo?
Is the crossing direct to Palermo?

Sì.
Yes.

Spɛro che il mare sarà calmo.
I hope the sea will be calm.

---

[1] § 75 (40).   [2] **riservare** = **prenotare**.

Perchè? Soffre il mal di mare?

Why? Do you get seasick (lit. "suffer from seasickness")?

Sì, ma soltanto quando il mare è mosso.

Yes, but only when the sea is rough.

Ɛcco il Suo biglietto. Sabato alle diciannove può[3] andare a bordo.

Here's your ticket. You can go on board on Saturday at 7:00 P.M.

Grazie. Buon giorno.

Thank you. (Good-bye.)

Prɛgo. Buon giorno.

You're welcome. (Good-bye.)

NOTE

1. **Il *Vulcano* = il piroscafo** (or **il vapore**) ***Vulcano***. Names of boats are masculine because **piroscafo** or **vapore** (*steamer*) *is* understood.

2. Other vocabulary: **traghetto** (or **nave traghetto** *f.*), *ferry-boat*; **aliscafo**, *hydrofoil boat*; **ponte** *m. deck*; **passerɛlla** *gangplank*; **crociɛra** *f. cruise*; **prenotazione** *f. reservation.*

---

[3] From **potere**. § 75 (21).

Un giro per la Sicília

A Tour Through Sicily

(Al portiɛre dell'albɛrgo) Mi dà un consíglio per favore?
> (*To the hotel concierge*) *Could I ask you for your advice* (*lit. "can you give me advice"*), *please?*

Prɛgo.
> *Go ahead* (*lit. "I beg you"*).

Sono arrivato a Palɛrmo due giorni fa, e ora vorrɛi vi*s*itare il rɛsto della Sicília.
> *I arrived in Palermo two days ago, and now I would like to visit the rest of Sicily.*

Ha già vi*s*itato la città e i dintorni?
> *Have you already been around the city and its outskirts?*

Sì.
> *Yes.*

Ha una m*a*cchina?
> *Do you have a car?*

Nɔ.
> *No.*

Allora puɔ fare il giro dell'*i*sola in trɛno o in autopullman.[1]
> *Then you can go on a tour of the island by train or by bus.*

Cɔsa mi consíglia?
> *What would you suggest?*

---

[1] **in trɛno** (**in autopullman**) = **col trɛno** (**coll'autopullman**), *by train* (*by bus*).

Vada[2] in autopullman. Ci sono dei giri turistici in autopullman di una settimana.

> *Go by bus. They have some one-week bus tours (lit. "for
> tourists").*

Io vorrei visitare i templi[3] di Segesta, di Selinunte e di Agri-
gento.

> *I would like to visit the temples at (lit. "of") Segesta,
> Selinunte, and Agrigento.*

Senz' altro. C'è un giro turistico che visita questi antichi
templi greci, e che va anche a Siracusa e a Piazza Armerina.

> *(You) definitely (should). There's a tour that goes to the
> (lit. "those") ancient Greek temples (you mentioned) and
> to Siracusa and Piazza Armerina as well.*

Siracusa m'interessa molto. Che cosa c'è a Piazza Armerina?

> *Siracusa really interests me. What is there in Piazza
> Armerina?*

C'è una villa romana con dei magnifici mosaici che rappre-
sentano varie fasi della vita romana del quarto secolo avanti
Cristo.

> *There's a Roman villa with beautiful mosaics that show
> (lit. "represent") different sides of Roman life in the fourth
> century B.C.*

Benissimo. L'autopullman si ferma anche a Taormina?

> *Tremendous. Does the bus stop at Taormina also?*

Sì. E poi ritorna a Palermo.

> *Yes. And then it comes back to Palermo.*

È proprio quello che volevo. Dove posso[4] prenotare un posto?

> *That's exactly what I wanted. Where can I reserve a place?*

---

[2] From **andare**. § 75 (1).   [3] The singular form is **tempio** *m*.   [4] From **potere**
§ 75 (21).

Ci penso io; o, se preferisce, c'è un'agenzia di viaggi qui vicino.

> *I'll take care of that (lit. "I will think of that"); or, if you like, there's a travel agency near here.*

Grazie.

> *Thank you.*

Prego.

> *You're welcome.*

NOTE

autopullman *m.* is used mainly with reference to sight-seeing and intercity buses.

In un caffè

In a Café

Ah, signor Brown, come sta? Quando è ritornato[1] a Roma?
> *Well, Bob (lit. "Mr Brown"), how are you? When did you get back (to Rome)?*

Iɛri sera. Domani parto per Firɛnze.
> *Last night. Tomorrow I'm leaving for Florence.*

Fermiamoci[2] a questo caffè.[3] Io hɔ molta sete.[4]
> *Let's stop at this café. I'm very thirsty.*

Anch'io.
> *So am I.*

Preferisce sedersi qui fuɔri?
> *Do you prefer to sit outside here?*

Sì. Dentro farà[5] trɔppo caldo.
> *Yes. It's probably too warm inside.*

Sediamoci[2] a questo tavolino all'ombra.
> *Let's sit down at this table in the shade.*

(Chiamando il cameriɛre) Cameriɛre!
(Chiamando la cameriɛra) Signorina! (Signora!)
> *(Calling the waiter) Waiter!*
> *(Calling the waitress) Waitress (lit. "Miss," "madam")!*

Vɛngo subito. Che cɔsa desiderano?
> *I'll be right there. What would you like?*

---

[1] § 43*b*. [2] § 35. [3] **caffè = bar** *m.* [4] § 66*a*. [5] Future of probability. § 45*d*. **Fare caldo,** *to be warm* (of the weather). § 67*b*.

Mi pɔrti un'aranciata fresca.
Bring me a cold orangeade.

E a me pɔrti un gelato di fragola.
And bring me a dish of strawberry ice cream.

Benⁱssimo, signori. Desⁱderano anche qualche pasta?[6] Abbiamo delle paste fresche[7] squisite.
Fine, (gentlemen). Would you like a few pastries too? We have some delicious (lit. "exquisite") fresh pastries.

Ci pɔrti due bignè.
Bring us two cream puffs.

C'ɛ molta gɛnte in giro ɔggi.
There are a lot of people out today.

Ɛ vero. Ɛ una bellⁱssima giornata.
That's right. It's a very beautiful day.

Ɛcco il cameriɛre.
Here's the waiter.

Ha fatto prɛsto.
It didn't take him long (lit. "he has done quickly").

Il gelato ɛ squisito. Com'ɛ l'aranciata?
The ice cream is delicious. How's the orangeade?

Non c'ɛ male.[8] I bignè[9] sono deliziosi.
Not bad. The cream puffs taste wonderful (lit. "are delicious").

(Chiama) Cameriɛre!
(Calls) Waiter!

Desⁱderano altro?
Would you like something else?

Il conto, per favore.
Check, please.

[6] § 19. [7] § 12. [8] **non c'ɛ male = discreto.** [9] § 7*d.*

Il serv*izio* è compreso?
> *Is service included?*

Sì, signori.
> *Yes (gentlemen).*

NOTE

1. In a hotel, **bar** corresponds to the American *bar*. Other vocabulary: **pasticceria**, *pastry shop*; **gelateria**, *icecream parlor*.

2. One may prefer a table **al sole**, *in the sunshine*, or **al fresco**, *in a cool place*.

3. Useful vocabulary for drinks: **ghiacciata** (= **diacciata**), *iced*; **ghi*a*ccio**, *ice*; **cann*u*ccia**, *straw*.

4. An alternative word for **gelato** is **sorbetto**, *sherbet*.

5. **mattinata**, *morning*; **serata**, *evening*; **nottata**, *night*. As contrasted with **giorno**, **mattina**, **sera**, **n**ɔ**tte**, the longer forms are descriptive and refer to the length, beauty, etc., of the day, morning, etc.

Il viaggio in treno

The Train Trip

■ **Allo sportello d'informazioni**   *At the Information Window*

Scusi. A che ora parte il treno per Firenze?
Excuse me. What time does the train leave for Florence?

Ci sono diversi treni. Vuole partire di mattina, nel pomeriggio, o di sera?
There are several trains. Do you want to leave in the morning, the afternoon, or the evening?

A che ora parte il rapido?[1]
What time does the express leave?

C'è un rapido alle tredici.
There is an express train at one P.M.

A che ora arriva a Firenze?
What time does it arrive in Florence?

Alle diciassette; cioè, se non è in ritardo.
Five in the evening; that is, if it's not late.

Porta un vagone ristorante?[2]
Does it have a diner?

Sì, signore.
Yes, sir.

Benissimo. Dove compro il biglietto?
Fine. Where do I buy my ticket?

---

[1] **rapido = espresso = diretto**, *express* (*train*).   [2] **vagone** *m.* (**carrozza** *or* **vettura**)- **letti**, *Pullman*.

Allo sportɛllo nʊmero diɛci.

At window number ten.

Grazie. Ah, dimenticavo.[3] Puɔ darmi un orario?

Thank you. Oh, I nearly forgot. Would you give me a timetable?

Con molto piacere. Ɛccolo.

Certainly (lit. "with much pleasure"). Here you are (lit. "here it is").

Mille grazie.

Many thanks.

NƆTE

1. **in trɛno** = **in ferrovia,** *by rail.*

2. Another expression of time: **di nɔtte,** *at night.*

3. Other kinds of train: **misto,** *carrying passengers and freight;* **trɛno mɛrci,** *freight train.*

4. The opposite of **in ritardo** is **in orario,** *on time,* or **in anticipo,** *ahead of schedule.*

[3] **dimenticare,** *to forget.*

La biglietteria

The Ticket Office

È qui l'ufficio dei biglietti?
> *Is this the ticket office?*

Sì, signore.
> *Yes, sir.*

Un biglietto per Firenze.
> *A ticket to Florence.*

Di che classe: prima, o seconda?
> *What class: first or second?*

Di prima.
> *First.*

Di corsa semplice o di andata e ritorno?
> *One-way or round-trip?*

Per quanto tempo è valido il biglietto di andata e ritorno?
> *How long is the round-trip ticket good for (or valid)?*

Per quindici giorni.
> *Fifteen days.*

Allora non mi conviene[1] perchè intendo[2] restare a Firenze venti giorni.
> *Then it won't do, because I intend to stay twenty days in Florence.*

---

[1] **convenire**, *to be worth while, suit*, etc., is conjugated like **venire**, t*o come.* §75 (38).   [2] **intendere** = **avere l'intenzione di** = **fare conto di**, *to plan, intend.*

Come desidera.
> *Just as you like* (or *As you wish*).

Quanto costa il biglietto di prima classe?
> *How much does the first-class ticket cost?*

Molto più del biglietto di seconda. Sui biglietti d'andata e ritorno c'è uno sconto del 20 (venti) per cento.
> *Much more than a second-class ticket. There's a reduction of twenty percent on round-trip tickets.*

Mi dispiace ma non posso approfittare di questa tariffa speciale.
> *I'm sorry but I can't take advantage of the (lit. "that") special rate.*

Ecco il biglietto e il resto.
> *Here's your ticket and your change.*

L'ufficio di spedizione (dei bagagli)

The Baggage Room

Facchino, per favore porti tutti questi bagagli all'ufficio di spedizione.
Porter, would you (lit, "please") carry all these bags to the baggage room.

(Arrivando) Vuole spedire un baule?
(Arriving) Do you need to check a trunk?

No, non ho nessun[1] baule. Ho queste tre valige e questo pacco.
No. I don't have a trunk. I've got these three suitcases and this package.

Sta bene. Pesiamo tutto.
O.K. Let's weigh it all.

A quanti chili[2] ho diritto?
How many kilos am I allowed?

Ha diritto a trenta chili. Vediamo. Quindici chili in tutto.
You're allowed thirty kilos. Let's see. Fifteen kilos in all.

Allora non c'è eccedenza.
Then there's no overweight (lit. "excess").

E Lei non mi deve[3] niente. Ecco i Suoi scontrini.
And you don't owe me a thing. Here are your checks (or stubs).

---

[1] **nessun (nessuno, nessuna, nessun')** is used like the indefinite article. § 3.
[2] **chilo (grammo)** = 2⅕ pounds. § 78.   [3] **dovere**, *to owe, must, have to.* § 75 (13).

Grazie. Può spedire i miei bagagli direttamente all'albergo?
Thank you. Can you send my luggage directly to the hotel?

Certamente.
Sure.

Allora Le lascio il mio indirizzo.
Then I'll leave my address here with you.

Non perda gli scontrini.
Don't lose the checks.

Non dubiti.
I won't (lit. "do not doubt").

Inoltre, le valige hanno le Sue iniziali.
Anyhow, your bags have your initials on them.

È vero. Ora corro al treno perchè fra pochi minuti parte.[4]
That's right. Now I'll run to the train because it leaves in a few minutes.

NOTE

spedire actually means *to send, ship;* additional vocabulary: **spedizioniere** *m., baggage room clerk.*

[4] Present for future. § 45a.

Nel deposito di bagagli

In the Checkroom

Vorrei[1] lasciar[2] qui questi bagagli.
> *I'd like to leave this luggage here.*

Benissimo.
> *O.K.*

A che ora chiudete?
> *What time do you close?*

Chiudiamo alle undici di sera.
> *We close at 11 P.M.*

Va bene. Quanto si paga[3] per ogni collo?
> *All right. How much do I pay for each piece?*

Non molto.
> *Not much.*

Pago ora o al[4] ritirarli?
> *Do I pay now or when I get it?*

Ora, per favore.
> *Now, please.*

Ecco.
> *Here you are.*

Ecco gli scontrini.
> *Here are your stubs.*

---

[1] Conditional of **volere**, *to want.* § 75 (40).   [2] § 14*a.*   [3] **pagare**, *to pay*; **si paga,** *is paid, one pays.* § 59*b.*   [4] **al** + inf. § 55*a.*

Che cosa faccio[5] se perdo gli scontrini?
What do I do if I lose the stubs?

In tal caso Lei dovrà dichiarare il contenuto delle valige e presentare le chiavi.
In that case you'll have to declare the contents of the suit-cases and present the keys.

Meno male che ho due chiavi per ogni valigia.
It's a good thing I have two keys for each suitcase.

Attenzione a non perderle tutt'e due!
Watch that you don't lose both of them!

Grazie del consiglio.
Thanks for the advice.

NOTE

che faccio? *what shall I do?* **che facciamo?** *what shall we do?* **che gli dico?** *what shall I tell him?*

[5] § 45a.

Sul marciapiɛde della stazione

On the Railway Platform

Dɛvo far prɛsto.[1] Non hɔ che cinque minuti. (Entrando) Scusi, signore.   Dov'ɛ il trɛno per Firɛnze?
> *I've got to hurry. I've only got five minutes. (Entering) Excuse me (sir). Where's the train to Florence?*

Ɛ quel trɛno là. Ɛ il numero sɛi.
> *It's that train there. It's number six.*

Va a Firɛnze anche Lɛi?
> *Are you going to Florence too?*

Sì. Se vuɔle, possiamo sedere vicini.
> *Yes. We can sit together if you like.*

Con piacere. Io volevo un posto d'angolo per poter osservare il paesaggio, ma in compagnia preferisco parlare.
> *That would be nice (lit. "with pleasure"). I wanted a corner seat so that I could look at the countryside (lit. "to be able to observe the landscape"), but with company I prefer to chat.*

Anch'io. Saliamo. Il trɛno sta per partire.
> *So do I. Let's get on. The train's about to leave.*

Ɛcco due ɔttimi[2] posti.
> *Here are two excellent seats.*

Prima di tutto vɔglio mettere il cappɛllo e il soprabito nella rete.
> *First of all I want to put my hat and my overcoat on the rack.*

---

[1] **fare prɛsto = affrettarsi.**   [2] § 24a.

Sa se è permesso[3] fumare qui?

Do you know whether smoking's allowed here?

No. Qui è vietato[4] fumare.

No. Smoking's forbidden here.

Allora dove possiamo fumare?

Then where can we smoke?

Nello scompartimento per fumatori.

In the smoking compartment.

In tal caso fumeremo più tardi.

In that case we'll smoke later.

(Un ragazzo che vende spuntini) Panini, acqua minerale, birra. . .

(A boy who is selling snacks) Rolls (stuffed), mineral water, beer. . . .

Ancora non ho fame.

I'm not hungry yet.

Nemmeno io.

I'm not either.

NOTE

marciapiede = piattaforma; biglietto d'entrata, *platform ticket, visitor's ticket.*

[3] **permettere,** *to permit, allow,* is conjugated like **mettere,** *to put.* § 75
(18).   [4] **vietato = proibito.**

In trεno

On the Train

Non spɔrga[1] la tεsta dal finestrino.
Don't stick your head out of the window.

Perchè?
Why?

Perchè è proibito spɔrgersi.
Because leaning out is forbidden.

Se è così, chiudo subito il finestrino.
If that's so, I'll close the window right away.

Fa bεne. C'è corrεnte ed entra molta pɔlvere.
I don't blame you (lit. "you do well"). There's a draft and a lot of dust is coming in.

E abbassiamo la tendina. Il sole dà nɔia.[2]
And let's lower the shade. The sun is annoying.

Benissimo. Evidentemente questa carrɔzza non ha l'aria condizionata.
Fine. This coach doesn't seem to be air-conditioned.

(Controllore[3]) Il Suo biglietto, per favore.
(Conductor) Your ticket please.

O dove hɔ messo[4] il biglietto?
Oh! where've I put my ticket?

Non lo trɔva?[5]
Can't you find it?

---

[1] Present subjunctive of **spɔrgere**. § 71.   [2] **dare nɔia (a)**, *to bother, annoy.*
[3] **controllore = bigliettaio.**   [4] From **mettere.** § 75 (18).   [5] **trovare,** *to find.*

Un momento, per favore. Ah, sì. L'hɔ messo in questa tasca.
Ɛccolo.

> *Just a minute, please. Oh, yes. I've put it away in this
> pocket. Here it is.*

Se il signore desidera mangiare qualcɔsa, la carrɔzza-ristorante
è avanti.

> *If you want to eat anything, the diner is forward.*

Grazie. Ci[6] vado subito. Hɔ fame.[7]

> *Thank you. I'm going (there) right away. I'm hungry.*

NOTE

1. The word for *window* is **finɛstra**; but the window of a
coach, automobile, etc., is **finestrino** (lit. "small window"). See 17*b*.

2. The word for *curtain* is **tɛnda**; but the curtain of a
coach, automobile, etc., is **tendina**.

3. The English word *can* is often not expressed in Italian:
non lo vedo, *I can't see him*; **non lo trɔvo**, *I can't find him*; **lo sɛnte?**
can you hear it?

4. The opposite of **avanti**, as used here, is **indiɛtro**.

[6] § 38.   [7] For several idioms with the verb **avere** see § 66*a*.

Oggɛtti perduti

Lost (and Found) Articles

Hɔ dimenticato una valigia in trɛno.
> *I left (lit. "forgot") a suitcase on the train.*

Come ɛra? Di che colore ɛra?
> *What was it like? What color was it?*

Ɛra (di color) caffɛ̀, con un cartellino rosso.
> *It was brown, with a red label (on it).*

Quant'ɛra grande?
> *How big was it?*

Ɛra lunga così, e larga così.
> *It was this (lit. "so") long, and this wide.*

Dove l'aveva messa?[1]
> *Where had you put it?*

Sul portabagaglio del mio scompartimento.
> *On the overhead rack of my compartment.*

Benissimo. Ɛcco la Sua valigia. L'apra e veda se manca qualcɔsa.
> *All right. Here's your suitcase. Open it and see if anything's missing.*

Manca un portafɔglio dove avevo il mio passapɔrto, e del denaro.
> *My billfold, with (lit. "in which I had") my passport and some money (in it), is missing.*

---

[1] From **mɛttere.** §§ 75 (18), 43*a*.

Non si ɛcciti, signore. Si calmi.[2]
> *Don't get excited, (sir). Take it easy.*

Che faccio ora? Non hɔ che pɔche lire in tasca.
> *What am I going to do now? I've only got a few lire in my pocket.*

Telɛfono subito al capostazione.
> *I'll phone the stationmaster right away.*

Ci vorrà[3] molto? Hɔ fretta.
> *Will it take long? I'm in a hurry.*

Ritorni fra mɛzz'ora.
> *Come back in half an hour.*

Non mancherɔ.[4]
> *I sure will (lit. "I will not fail").*

NƆTE

1. The question **come ɛra?** could have been posed in the present: **com'ɛ?** *what is it like?* To ask dimensions of objects: **di che grandezza ɛ?** *how big is it?* (lit. "of what size is it?"); **quanto** (or **come**) ɛ grande (**piccolo, largo, corto, lungo, stretto,** etc.)? *how big (small, wide, short, long, narrow, etc.) is it?* or ɛ **molto grande?** *is it very large?*, etc. The answers may be: ɛ **lungo (largo) un mɛtro,** *it is a meter long (wide);* **ha un'altezza (una profondità) di cinquecɛnto piɛdi,** *it is five hundred feet high (deep).*

2. An alternative expression: **non si ɛcciti = non si alteri,** *don't get excited.*

3. **In tasca** may be replaced by **addɔsso,** *on me.*

---

[2] **calmarsi = tranquillizzarsi,** *to be calm, calm down.* § 71.   [3] Future of **volere.**
[4] §73a.

Il Palio di Siena

The Palio of Siena

Il primo luglio vado a Siena.
  I'm going to Siena on the first of July.

Ci va per affari?
  Are you going on business?

No. Ci vado con la famiglia. Andiamo a vedere il Palio.
  No. I'm going with my family. We're going to see the Palio.

Che cosa è il Palio?
  What is the Palio?

Non lo sa?[1] È una famosa corsa di cavalli che risale al Medio Evo.
  Don't you know? It's a famous horse race that goes back to the Middle Ages.

Non è una corsa di cavalli come tutte le altre?
  Is it different from other horse races (lit. "it's not a horse race like all the others")?

No. Siena è divisa[2] in diverse contrade, ed ogni contrada ha la sua bandiera, i suoi colori e il suo cavallo.
  Yes. Siena is divided into a number of districts, and each district has its banner, its colors, and its horse.

In quante contrade è divisa Siena?
  How many districts is Siena divided into?

---

[1] From **sapere**. § 75 (28).   [2] Irregular past participle of **dividere**, *to divide*.

In diciassette, ma solamente dieci partecipano alla corsa, che ha luogo nella Piazza del Campo il due luglio e il sedici agosto.

> *Seventeen, but only ten take part in the race, which is held in the Piazza del Campo on July 2 and August 16.*

Dev'essere molto bella.

> *It must be very beautiful.*

Pittoresca. Prima della corsa c'è un corteo a cui prendono parte i rappresentanti delle contrade vestiti in costumi di molti colori, i fantini a cavallo, e il Carroccio dell'antica repubblica di Siena.

> *It's picturesque. Before the race there's a procession and the district representatives dressed in multicolored costumes, the jockeys on horseback, and the Carroccio of the old republic of Siena take part in it.*

Che cos'è il Carroccio?

> *What is the Carroccio?*

È un carro tirato da cavalli che era usato in guerra dalle antiche repubbliche italiane, e da cui sventolava la bandiera del comune.

> *It's a horse-drawn cart that was used in war by the old Italian republics, and from which the flag of the commune was flown.*

Allora ha un significato storico.

> *Then it has a historical significance.*

Precisamente. Ora sul Carroccio ci[3] mettono il premio che sarà dato al vincitore: il Palio.

> *Exactly. Now they place on the Carroccio the prize which will be given to the winner: the Palio (cloth).*

Dev'essere una corsa molto interessante.

> *It must be a very interesting race.*

[3] § 37.

Emozionant*i*ssima. Specialmente per i senesi.
Very thrilling. Especially for the people of Siena.

Per il momento sono molto occupato, ma farò di tutto per vedere il P*a*lio del sedici agosto.
At the moment I'm very busy, but I'll make every effort to see the Palio on the sixteenth of August.

NOTE

1. Except for *first*, which is **primo**, the cardinal numerals are used in dates. *August 5 =* **il 5 (c*i*nque) di agosto,** etc.

2. **affari** (sing. **affare**) is generally used in the plural: **un u*o*mo d'affari,** *a business man;* **come vanno gli affari?** *how's business?* **gli affari vanno b*e*ne (male),** *business is good (bad).*

4

Vita quotidiana

Daily Life

La lɛttera di raccomandazione

The Letter of Recommendation

C'ɛ il signor Bianchi?
> *Is Mr. Bianchi in?*

Sì, signore. Chi dɛvo[1] annunziare?
> *Yes, sir. May I tell him who is calling (lit. "whom shall I announce")?*

Ɛcco il mio biglietto da [2] visita.
> *Here is my (calling) card.*

Favorisca di passare e d'aspettare un momento.
> *Please come in and wait a minute.*

Buon giorno. Mi scusi di averla fatta aspettare.
> *How do you do. Excuse me for having kept you waiting.*

Io sono John Brown. Questa ɛ una lɛttera del signor Solari.
> *I'm John Brown. This is a letter from Mr. Solari.*

Ah, il mio caro amico. Come sta?
> *Oh, my dear friend. How is he?*

Benissimo. Le manda tanti saluti.
> *Fine. He sends you greetings.*

Permette? (Leggɛndo) «Ti sarò grato d'ogni attenzione che farai al mio amico—, portatore della presɛnte.» Ebbɛne, sono felicissimo di fare la Sua conoscɛnza.
> *Will you excuse me? (Reading) "I shall be grateful to you for any kindness you show my friend ——, bearer of this letter." Well, I'm very happy to know you.*

---

[1] From **dovere**. § 65*b*.   [2] § 62*c*.

Il piacere è mio, creda.
> *The pleasure is mine, believe me.*

Vɛnga a mangiare con noi una serə. Quanto tɛmpo si trattiɛne?[3]
> *Come and have dinner with us one evening. How long do you expect to stay?*

Soltanto tre giorni.
> *Only three days.*

Che giorno è lɪbero?
> *What day are you free?*

Che giorno è ɔggi?
> *What day is today?*

Ɔggi è martedì, due lᴜglio.
> *Today is Tuesday, July 2.*

Vediamo. Domani vado al teatro, e dopo domani dɛvo vedere cɛrti amici. Venerdì sono lɪbero.
> *Let's see. Tomorrow I'm going to the theater, and the day after tomorrow I am to see some friends. I'll be free Friday.*

Benɪssimo. Vɛnga venerdì e conoscerà anche la mia famɪglia.
> *Fine. Come Friday and you will meet my family also.*

Grazie. Mi dà l'indirizzo di casa Sua?
> *Thank you. Would you give me your home address?*

Cɛrto. Via Sardegna 15 (quɪndici).
> *Certainly. 15 Sardegna Street.*

Grazie. Allora a venerdì sera.
> *Thank you. See you Friday evening, then.*

Arrivederci.
> *See you then.*

---

[3] **trattenersi**, *to stay*, *linger*, is conjugated like **tenere**. § 75 (34).

NOTE

1.   There are two idiomatic expressions involving "home" in this dialogue: **c'è** is used alone for **c'è in casa**; **di casa Sua** is used for **della Sua casa**.

2.   **Conoscere** means *to meet* as well as *to know, be acquainted with*; but the past tenses have restricted meanings: **lo conobbi (ieri)**, *I met him (yesterday)*; **lo conoscevo**, *I knew him, used to know him*.

3.   In expressing dates, except for the first day of the month, which is always **il primo**, the other days are expressed by the cardinal numbers: **il due**, **il tre**, etc.

Affittando un appartamento

Renting an Apartment

Permesso?
> *May I come in?*

Avanti!
> *Come in!*

Buɔn giorno. S'accɔmodi. Cɔsa des*i*dera?
> *Good morning. Won't you sit down. What can I do for you?*

Vorrɛi affittare un appartamento.
> *I'd like to rent an apartment.*

Al cɛntro o in periferia?
> *Downtown or on the outskirts of town?*

Al cɛntro. Preferisco un appartamento tranquillo.
> *Downtown. I prefer a quiet apartment.*

Quante stanze Le occɔrrono?
> *How many rooms do you need?*

Almeno sɛi: due c*a*mere, stanza da pranzo, salɔtto, bagno, cucina, e una cameretta per la dɔnna di servizio.
> *At least six: two bedrooms, dining room, living room, bath, kitchen, and a small bedroom for the maid.*

Abbiamo un grazioso appartamento che fa prɔprio per Lɛi.
> *We have an attractive apartment that will meet your needs (lit. "which will do exactly for you").*

Ɛ̀ lontano dal cɛntro?
> *Is it far from downtown?*

A due passi.
Only a short distance.

S'intende che l'appartamento è completamente mobiliato.
The apartment is completely furnished, of course.

Sì. Eccetto la biancheria e l'argenteria a cui dovrà provvedere Lei stesso.
Yes. Except for the linen and silver, which you will have to supply yourself.

Che comodità ci sono?
What comes with it (lit. "what conveniences are there")?

C'è il frigorifero, la cucina elettrica, il lavastoviglie, la lavatrice e l'asciugatrice, e l'aspirapolvere.
There's a refrigerator, an electric stove, a dishwasher, a washer and dryer, and a vacuum cleaner.

Benissimo.
Fine.

E poi c'è un bagno, un mezzo bagno e una veduta magnifica.
And then there's a full bath, a half bath, and a magnificent view.

Qual è il prezzo d'affitto?
How much is the rent?

Aspetti che prendo il listino degli affitti.
Wait, I'll get the rental list.

NOTE

1. Alternative ways of saying **affittare** are: **prendere in affitto** or **prendere a pigione.**

2. Other parts of the house: **corridoio,** *corridor;* **soffitta,** *attic;* **cantina,** *cellar;* **scale** *f. pl., stairs;* **ascensore** *m., elevator.*

3. **mobile** *m., a piece of furniture;* **mobili** *m. pl., furniture* (in general) = **mobilia** *f. sing.*

4. Linen includes: **lenzuɔlo** (*pl.* **le lenzuɔla**), *sheet*; **fɛdera,** *pillowcase*; **tovaglia,** *tablecloth*; **tovagliɔlo,** *napkin*; **asciugamano,** *towel.*

5. Silver includes: **cucchiɑio,** *spoon*; **cucchiaino,** *teaspoon*; **coltɛllo,** *knife*; **forchetta,** *fork.*

6. Other vocabulary for the kitchen: **cucina a gas,** *gas stove*; **acquɑio,** *sink*; **rubinetto,** *faucet* = **cannɛlla dell'acqua.**

7. Other vocabulary for the bathroom: **vasca,** *tub*; **dɔccia,** *shower*; **gabinetto,** *toilet*

Nella libreria

At the Bookstore

Saprɛbbe dirmi se c'è una libreria qu*i* vicino?
Could you tell me whether there's a bookstore near here?

Ce ne sono tre, ma la migliore è in Via Mazzini.
There are three of them, but the best is on Mazzini Street.

Gr*a*zie. Da che parte è Via Mazzini?
Thank you. Which direction is Mazzini Street?

È in questa direzione. Segua questa via fino all'*a*ngolo e pɔi
vɔlti a dɛstra. Non puɔ *s*bagliare.
*It's this way. Follow this street to the corner and then turn
right. You can't go wrong.*

Mille gr*a*zie. (Attraversando la via) C*a*spita! Per pɔco quella
m*a*cchina m'investiva. Che mɔdo di guidare! Ɛccomi arrivato.
*Thank you very much. (Crossing the street) Wow! That
car nearly ran over me. What terrible drivers (lit. "what
way of driving")! . . . Here I am.*

Il signore des*i*dera?
What would you like?

Des*i*dero comprare il romanzo che ha vinto il prɛmio Viareg-
gio[1] . . . ma non ric*ɔ*rdo il t*i*tolo . . . l'hɔ sulla punta della l*i*ngua.
*I want to buy the novel that won the Viareggio prize . . . but
I don't remember the title. . . . I've got it on the tip of my
tongue.*

[1] A yearly literary prize.

Si riferisce forse al romanzo intitolato: «Montagne verdi»?

> *Maybe you mean (lit. "are referring to") the novel entitled "Green Mountains"?*

Esattamente.

> *That's it (lit. "exactly").*

Non ci restano che poche copie.

> *We only have a few copies left.*

Me lo vuole mostrare?

> *Will you show it to me?*

Eccolo. Altro?

> *Here it is. Anything else?*

Sì. Vorrei una guida e una pianta della città, e un dizionarietto tascabile.[2]

> *Yes. I'd like a guidebook and a plan of the city, and a little pocket dictionary.*

Questi sono i migliori e i meno costosi.

> *These are the best and the least expensive.*

(Sfogliandoli) Li prendo. Me li involge in un pezzo di carta, per favore?

> *(Glancing through them) I'll take them. Will you wrap them up, please?*

Glieli metto in questo sacchetto di carta insieme al nostro ultimo catalogo delle opere nazionali e straniere.

> *I'll put them in this little paper bag with our latest catalogue of domestic and foreign works.*

NOTE

1.   *library* is **biblioteca**; **libri usati**, *secondhand books.*

2.   Other literary vocabulary: **commedia**, *comedy*; **racconto** or **novella**, *short story*; **saggio**, *essay*; **storia**, *history, story*; **poesia**, *poetry*; **volume** *m.*, *volume.*

3.   *map* is **carta geografica.**

[2] **dizionario,** *dictionary* (§ 17b); **tasca,** *pocket,* **tascabile,** *pocket (adj.).*

Nel negozio di scarpe

In the Shoe Store

Desidero un paio di scarpe come quelle che sono in vetrina.
I want a pair of shoes like the ones in the window.

Benissimo, signore. Che numero porta?
Fine, sir. What size do you take?

Non ricordo.[1] Non sono sicuro.
I don't remember. I'm not sure.

In tal caso Le prendo la misura del piede. Il (numero) quarantadue.
In that case I'll measure your foot (lit. "take the measure of your foot"). Size 42.

Provi questo paio. Ecco il calzante.[2]
Try on this pair. Here's the shoehorn.

Mi vanno un po' strette. Stringono al collo del piede.[3]
They're a bit tight. They pinch on the instep.

Allora provi queste.
Then try these.

Queste sembrano un po' grandi.
These seem a bit big.

Aspetti un momento. Porto diversi modelli e Lei sceglierà.
Wait a minute. I'll bring several models so you can choose.

---

[1] non ricordo il numero = non mi ricordo del numero.   [2] calzante = calzatoio = calzascarpe *m.*   [3] collo = fiocca.

Mi piacciono[4] questi mocassini di pɛlle nera con la fíbbia.
> *I like these black leather moccasins with the buckle.*

Ha buɔn gusto. Le stanno molto bɛne.
> *You have good taste. They look very good on you.*

Sono veramente cɔmodi.
> *They're really comfortable.*

Glieli metto in una scatola?
> *Shall I put them in a box?*

Nɔ, li incarti.
> *No, wrap them up.*

Come vuɔle.
> (*As you wish.*)

Sɛnta, dove pɔsso far mettere[5] le mɛzze suɔle e i tacchi a queste scarpe?
> *Tell me (lit. "listen"), where can I have half soles and heels put on these shoes?*

C'ɛ un calzolaio in questa via vicino all'angolo di Via Dante.
> *There's a shoemaker on this street near the corner of Dante Street.*

Grazie. Buɔn giorno.
> *Thank you. Good-bye.*

Buɔn giorno. Grazie a Lei.
> *Good-bye. Thank you.*

NOTE

1. Names of other parts of the foot are **dito** (**del piɛde**), *toe*; **alluce** *m.* or **dito grɔsso** (**del piɛde**), *big toe*; **tallone** *m.* or **calcagno**, *heel* (*of foot*), as opposed to **tacco**, *heel* (*of shoe*).

[4] § 61.   [5] § 67a.

2. Material for shoes: **cuoio**, *leather*; **pelle** *f.*, *skin, soft leather*; **raso**, *satin*; **di camoscio**, *suede*;

3. Other kinds of shoe: **scarpine dorate (argentate)**, *gold (silver) slippers*; **stivali** *m. pl.*, *boots*; **sandali** *m. pl.*, *sandals*.

4. *to sole*, **risolare**.

Dal barbiεre

At the Barber's

È il mio turno, o dεvo aspettare?
> *Is it my turn, or do I have to wait?*

È il Suo turno,[1] signore. Che cɔsa desidera?
> *It's your turn, sir. What would you like?*

Barba e capelli.
> *A shave and a haircut.*

(Insaponandogli la faccia) Le dà nɔia la radio?
> *(Lathering his face) Does the radio bother you?*

Nɔ, nɔ. Al contrario, mi piace la musica.
> *No. In fact (lit. "on the contrary"), I like music.*

(Più tardi) Come desidera i capelli?
> *(Later) How do you want your hair (cut)?*

Non trɔppo corti. Ɔggi i capelli lunghi sono di mɔda.
> *Not too short. Today long hair is fashionable.*

Sì, ma non così lunghi come[2] l'anno scorso.
> *Yes, but not as long as last year.*

Ha ragione.
> *You're right.*

Ɛcco fatto. Vuɔle che Le lavi i capelli?
> *There you are. Do you want me to wash your hair?*

No, grazie.
> *No, thank you.*

---

[1] **ora ὲ il Suo turno**=**ora tocca a Lεi.**   [2] § 21.

Il signore è servito.   Si accomodi alla cassa.

> *There we are (lit. "the gentleman is served"). Please pay the cashier.*

Va bene.   Questo è per Lei.

> *All right. This is for you.*

Grazie.

> *Thank you.*

Buon giorno.

> (*Good-bye.*)

Buon giorno.

> (*Good-bye.*)

NOTE

1. For *hairdresser*, one says **parrucchiere**.

2. *Whose turn is it?* = **A chi tocca?**

3. Other useful vocabulary: **fare (radere) la barba**, *to shave*; **fare (tagliare) i capelli**, *to give a haircut.*

4. **Accomodarsi** actually means *to make oneself comfortable*; in command forms it means *please come* (*in*) and *please go* (*in*), and also *won't you sit down?*

Nel salone di bellezza

In the Beauty Salon

Pɔsso farmi lavare i capelli[1] adɛsso,[2] o dɛvo fare un appuntamento?

Can I have my hair washed now, or do I need to make an appointment?

Se vuɔle, possiamo servirla subito, signorina. Prɛgo, si accɔmodi.

If you wish, we can take (lit. "serve") you right now (Miss). Come along please.

Tanto mɛglio. Prima mi faccia[3] uno shampoo.

That's even better (lit. "so much the better").   First give me a shampoo.

Pɔi vuɔle una messa in piɛga, vero?

Then you want me to set your hair, don't you?

Sì, per favore, ma non trɔppo ricci.

Yes, please, but not too curly.

Benissimo.

O.K.

Quanto ci vorrà[4] ad asciugare i capelli?

How long will it take to dry my hair?

Una mɛzz'oretta. Desidera una manicure?

About half an hour.   Would you like a manicure?

Sì, grazie. Preferisco il (color) rosso ciliɛgia.

Yes, thank you.   I prefer cherry red.

---

[1] 67a.   [2] **adɛsso = ora.**   [3] From **fare.** § 75 (15).   [4] From **volere.** § 75 (40).

Vuole che Le depiliamo le sopracciglia?[5]
Shall we pluck your eyebrows?

No.
No.

Benissimo. Ecco fatto.
Fine. There you are.

Ora mi occorre un rossetto, e della crema per la pelle.
Now I need a lipstick and some facecream.

Questo rossetto Le piacerà moltissimo.
You'll really like this lipstick.

Questa crema toglie anche le lentiggini?
Does this cream remove freckles too?

No, signorina. Eccone una per le lentiggini; va applicata tutti i giorni prima del trucco.
No (Miss). Here's one for freckles: it must be applied every day before the make-up.

Pago alla cassa?
Do I pay the cashier?

Sì, signorina.
Yes (Miss).

NOTE

1. The opposite of **tanto meglio** is **tanto peggio**, *so much the worse.*

2. Other vocabulary: **ricciolo**, *curl*; **piega**, *wave.*

3. **Manicure** more correctly means *manicurist*, although in this sense it has been replaced by the word **manicurista** *f.*

4. Other vocabulary: **ciglio** *m.*, *eyelash*; **labbro** *m.*, *lip.*

5. When followed by a past participle, **andare**, *to go*, conveys the meaning of obligation.

[5] § 7a (2)

Dal sarto

At the Tailor's

Buɔn giorno.   Vorrɛi comprare un *a*bito confezionato.
> *Good morning.   I would like to buy a (ready-made) suit.*

Ben*i*ssimo.
> *Fine.*

Preferisco un colore chiaro e una stɔffa leggɛra.
> *I prefer a light color and a lightweight material.*

Vuɔle la giacca a un pɛtto o a due pɛtti?
> *Do you want a single- or double-breasted jacket?*

A un pɛtto.   E i pantaloni sɛnza risvɔlto.
> *Single-breasted.   And I'd like the pants without a cuff.*

Vuɔle provarsi quest'*a*bito grigio?
> *Do you want to try on this gray suit?*

Questo non mi sta bɛne.[1]
> *This doesn't look good on me.*

Come nɔ!   Sembra fatto[2] appɔsta per Lɛi.   Si guardi allo spɛcchio.
> *Of course it does!   It seems to have been made especially for you.   Look at yourself in the mirror.*

Non vede che diɛtro la giacca fa molte piɛghe?   E i pantaloni[3] sono trɔppo stretti.
> *Don't you see that the jacket has a lot of wrinkles in the back?   And the pants are too tight.*

---

[1] It can also mean *it does not fit me well.*   [2] From **fare**. § 75 (15).   [3] **pantaloni** = **calzoni**.

Senta. Perchè non si fa un abito su misura? Abbiamo un sarto bravissimo.

> *Listen. Why don't you have a suit made to order? We have an excellent tailor.*

Sarà la miglior cosa.

> *That's probably the best thing.*

Osservi. Le piace[4] questa stoffa a righe?

> *Look. Do you like this striped material?*

Sì, ma preferisco questa a quadri.

> *Yes, but I prefer this checked material.*

(Il sarto gli prende le misure) Ecco fatto, signore.

> *(The tailor takes his measurements) There you are, sir.*

Quando sarà pronto?

> *When will it be ready?*

Fra due settimane. Può venire venerdì per la prima prova.

> *In two weeks. (You may) come on Friday for the first fitting.*

Desidera che paghi[5] in contanti?

> *Do you want me to pay cash?*

Non c'è fretta. Quando il signore desidera. La prego soltanto di versare una piccola anticipazione.

> *There's no hurry. Whenever you wish. All I ask is that you make a small down payment.*

S'intende. A venerdì.

> *Of course. See you Friday.*

Buona sera.

> *Good night.*

NOTE

Other vocabulary: **panciotto** = **corpetto** = **gilè** *m., vest:* **cappotto** = **soprabito**, *overcoat.*

---

[4] § 61.   [5] Subjunctive of **pagare**, *to pay.* § 48.

Dalla sarta

At the Dressmaker's

Buɔna sera signora. Come vede sono molto puntuale.
Good afternoon, (madam). I'm very punctual, as you see.

È vero. Le dispiace di aspettare un momentino? C'è una signorina che si sta provando un vestito.
That's true. Would you mind waiting a minute? There's a young lady here who's trying on a dress.

Le pare! Non hɔ fretta.
Of course not! I'm in no hurry.

(Pɔco dopo) Ora sono a Sua disposizione.
(A little later) Now I'm ready for you.

Vediamo come mi va[1] il vestito nuɔvo.
Let's see how my new dress fits me.

Se lo metta. Guardi. Le sta a pennɛllo.
Put it on. Look. It fits you like a glove.

Crede?
Do you think so?

Si guardi allo spɛcchio e si convincerà.
Look in the mirror and you'll be convinced.

Mi sembra che la gɔnna pɛnda[2] da una parte.
It seems to me that the skirt sags on one side.

---

[1] **mi va** (*or* **sta**) **bɛne**, *it fits me*; **mi sta bɛne**, *it becomes me.*   [2] **pɛnda** (**pɛndere**), present subjunctive. § 49.

Ha ragione. Non mi piace come sta.
You're right. I don't like the way it hangs.

Nemmeno a me. Sembra così larga.
Nor do I. It seems so wide.

Non si preoccupi; vedrà come l'accomoderemo. E ora proviamo le maniche.
Don't worry, we'll fix that (lit. "you will see how we shall fix it"). And now let's try the sleeves.

Sembrano un po' strette. Bisognerà allargarle.
They seem a little tight. They'll have to be let out.

Le spalle e il collo stanno a perfezione.
The shoulders and the neck are perfect.

Ha segnato le correzioni?
Have you marked the alterations?

Sì. Il vestito sarà pronto per dopo domani.
Yes. The dress will be ready the day after tomorrow.

Volevo mettermelo stasera, ma vuol dire che aspetterò.
I wanted to wear it this evening, but that means that I'll wait.

NOTE

1. **cucitrice** *f.*, *seamstress*; **modista,** *milliner.*

2. Other useful vocabulary: **piega,** *pleat*; **pieghettato,** *pleated*; **guarnizione** *f.*, *trimming*; **bottoni automatici** *m. pl.*, *snaps*; **chiusura lampo** *f.*, *zipper*; **ganci** (*m. pl.*) **e magliette** (*f. pl.*), *hooks and eyes*; **scollato,** *low-cut*; **disegno,** *pattern.*

3. Materials: **panni e tessuti,** *materials and fabrics*; **cotone** *m.*, *cotton*; **batista,** *batiste*; **merletto** or **trina,** *lace*; **lana,** *wool*; **lino,** *linen*; **raso,** *satin*; **seta,** *silk*; **velluto,** *velvet.*

4. A useful phrase: **voglio un vestito fatto su misura,** *I want a tailored suit.*

In un magazzino

In a Department Store

Scusi, dov'è il reparto uomo?
> *Excuse me, where is the men's department?*

È al terzo piano. L'ascensore è qui a destra, ma può salire anche in scala mobile.
> *On the third floor. The elevator is here on your right, but you may also go up on the escalator.*

(Ascensorista) Primo piano: reparto signora . . . secondo piano: mobili, tappeti, elettrodomestici . . . terzo piano: reparto uomo. . . .
> *(Elevator Operator) First floor: ladies' department . . . second floor: furniture, carpets, electrical appliances . . . third floor: men's department . . .*

Buon giorno.   Può aspettare un momento?
> *Good morning. Can you wait a moment?*

Faccia pure.   Non ho fretta.
> *Go right ahead. I'm not in a hurry.*

Finisco di servire questo signore.
> *I'll finish waiting on this gentleman.*

Darò uno sguardo a queste camicie e a queste cravatte.
> *I'll take a look at these shirts and ties.*

(Poco dopo) Ha trovato qualcosa di Suo gusto?
> *(After a while) Have you found something that appeals to you?*

Quanto còstano queste?

> *How much do these cost?*

Queste sono molto a buòn mercato ora. La nòstra liquidazione è cominciata appunto òggi. Che numero pòrta?

> *These are very cheap now. Our (clearance) sale has just begun today. What size do you wear?*

Il numero quindici (trentòtto).

> *Size fifteen (thirty-eight).*

Su queste camicie c'è uno sconto del venti per cento. Quante ne[1] vuòle? Mɛzza dozzina?

> *On these shirts there's a reduction of twenty percent. How many would you like? Half a dozen?*

Mi basta una camicia. Prɛndo questa azzurra a righe.

> *One shirt is enough. I'll take this blue striped one.*

Non ha bisogno di cravatte di seta, calzini di lana. . . . ?

> *Don't you need any silk ties, woolen socks . . . ?*

Non sò se hò abbastanza denaro con me. Tutto è così a buòn mercato!

> *I don't know whether I have enough money with me. Everything is so reasonable!*

(Aprɛndo il portafòglio) Nò, non hò abbastanza denaro. Pòsso scrivere un assegno?

> *(Opening his billfold) No, I've not got enough money. Can I write a check?*

Mi dispiace, ma non accettiamo assegni. Vendiamo soltanto a contanti.

> *I'm sorry, but we don't accept checks. We make only cash sales.*

Va bɛne. Pago alla cassa, vero? Da dove si ɛsce?

> *All right. I pay the cashier, don't I? How does one get out?*

[1] § 33a.

Di là, signore. L'ascensore è alla Sua destra.
That way, sir. The elevator is on your right.

Grazie.
Thank you.

NOTE

1. **magazzino** is often used in the plural, as in **grandi magazzini**; it also means *warehouse.* Other kinds of store: **negozio**, *store*; **bottega**, *shop*; **camiceria**, *haberdashery, men's store.*

2. Other kinds of sales: **occasione** *f.,* *bargain sale*; **liquidazione** *f., clearance sale.*

3. Size 15 (inches) would correspond to about 38 (centimeters) in countries using the metric system. § 78.

4. Other vocabulary for prices: **ribassare**, *to reduce (the price)*; **alzare**, *to raise (the price)*; **mercanteggiare**, *to haggle* (**tirare sul prezzo**).

In un'oreficeria

At the Jeweller's

Può accomodare[1] quest'orologio?
> *Can you repair this watch?*

Che ha?
> *What's the matter with it?*

Non va bɛne.   Un giorno va avanti, un giorno va indiɛtro; e ora s'ɛ̀ fermato.[2]
> *It doesn't run well. One day it's fast, another day it's slow; and now it's stopped.*

Lo carica regolarmente?
> *Do you wind it regularly?*

Tutti i[3] giorni.
> *Every day.*

Vediamo. Ɛ̀ rotta la mɔlla.
> *Let's see. The spring is broken.*

Può accomodarlo?
> *Can you fix it?*

Sì, ma non Le mɛrita conto. Perchè non compra un altro orolɔgio?
> *Yes, but it's not worthwhile. Why don't you buy another watch?*

Mi fa[4] uno sconto?
> *Will you give me a discount?*

---

[1] **accomodare = aggiustare = riparare.**   [2] § 74.   [3] **tutti i (tutte le),** *every* (plus noun).   [4] § 75 (15).

Va bɛne. Le faccio[4] lo sconto del venti per cɛnto.
> *All right. I'll give you a twenty percent discount.*

Preferirɛi un orolɔgio elɛttrico.
> *I'd prefer an electric watch.*

Guardi quant'ɛ carino[5] questo, signorina. Ɛ d'ɔro.
> *Look how nice this one is, (Miss). It's gold.*

Sì. Anche il cinturino ɛ molto bɛllo. Lo prɛndo.
> *Yes. The strap is really beautiful too. I'll take it.*

Vuɔle vedere anche un paio d'orecchini?
> *Would you like to see a pair of earrings also?*

Nɔ. Magari potrɛbbe[6] mostrarmi una collana di pɛrle.
> *No. Maybe you could show me a pearl necklace.*

Vere o coltivate?
> *Real or cultured?*

Coltivate. Le pɛrle vere cɔstano trɔppo.
> *Cultured. Real pearls cost too much.*

Attɛnda un momento. Prɛndo la collana che ɛ in vetrina.
> *Wait a minute. I'll get the necklace (which is) in the window.*

Sɛnta. Veramente ora ho fretta.[7] La metta da parte; ripasserɔ domani.
> *Listen. As a matter of fact I'm in a hurry now. Put it aside (for me); I'll come back tomorrow.*

Come desidera. Buɔna sera.
> *Fine (lit. "as you wish"). Good evening.*

Buɔna sera.
> *Good evening.*

NƆTE

1. **Orefice** *m.*, *goldsmith*; **oreficeria** = **gioielleria**, which actually means *jewelry store*; **gioiɛllo**, *jewel*; **orologeria**, *watchmaker's store*.

---

[5] **carino** = **grazioso**, *pretty.*   [6] §§ 75 (21), 64.   [7] § 66a.

2. **Orolɔgio da polso,** *wrist watch*; **sveglia,** *alarm clock.*

3. **Un orolɔgio d'ɔro (d'argɛnto, d'acciɑio inossidɑbile),** *a gold (silver, stainless steel) watch.*

4. Other kinds of precious stones: **brillante** *m.* = **diamante** *m.*, *diamond*; **corallo,** *coral*; **piɛtre preziose** *f. pl.*, *precious stones.*

Alla pɔsta

At the Post Office

Quanto cɔsta l'affrancatura di una lɛttera per l'ɛstero per pɔsta aɛrea?

What is the postage on a letter to foreign countries by airmail?

Duecɛnto ottanta lire.

Two hundred and eighty lire.

Ben*i*ssimo. Mi dia due francobolli per l'ɛstero e uno per l'intɛrno.

All right. Give me two stamps for foreign countries and one regular (lit. "for the interior").

Sono settecɛnto quaranta lire.

That's seven hundred forty lire.

Vorrɛi anche spedire questo pacco.

And I'd like to mail this package.

Ha dimenticato di scr*i*vere il nome e l'indirizzo del mittɛnte.

You forgot to write the name and address of the sender.

Non credevo che fosse[1] necess*a*rio.

I didn't think it was necessary.

Sì, signore, affinchè si pɔssa[2] resp*i*ngere la lɛttera se non si trɔva il destinat*a*rio.

Yes, sir, so that the letter can be returned if the addressee cannot be found.

[1] Past subjunctive of **ɛssere**. §§ 48, 54.   [2] Present subjunctive of **potere**. §§ 75 (21),   50*a*.

Questa lettera arriverà al destinatario lunedì prossimo se la spedisco per posta aerea?

Will this letter reach the addressee next Monday if I send it by airmail?

Sì, signore. Ci mette soltanto tre giorni ad arrivare.

Yes, sir. It only takes three days to get there.

E dove l'imposto?[3]

And where shall I mail it?

L'imposti nella buca di fronte.

Drop it in the mail box over there (lit. "facing us").

Qualche tempo fa mandai una lettera raccomandata a Bologna ma non è giunta[4] a destinazione.

Some time ago I sent a registered letter to Bologna, but it hasn't arrived at its destination.

Ha la ricevuta?

Have you got the receipt?

Sfortunatamente l'ho smarrita.

Unfortunately I've mislaid it.

A chi era indirizzata la lettera?

Who was the letter addressed to?

Al signor Andrea Galli ed aveva il mio nome sul dietro della busta.

Mr. Andrea Galli, and it had my name on the back of the envelope.

Favorisca d'aspettare un momento.

Wait a minute, please.

Mentre aspetto vado a vedere se c'è qualche lettera per me al fermo in posta.

While I'm waiting, I'll go and see if there are any letters for me at the General Delivery window.

---

[3] **impostare**=**imbucare**.   [4] From **giungere**=**arrivare**.   § 75 (16).

Mi fa il favore di vedere se ci sono lɛttere per me?
Will you please see if there are any letters for me?

Ɛcco la mia carta d'identità (il mio passapɔrto).
Here's my identification card (my passport).

Ci sono due lɛttere e queste stampe.
There are two letters and this printed matter.

Non c'ɛ̀ nessun pacco?
There's no package?

Nɔ, signore. Firmi questa ricevuta, per favore.
No, sir. Sign this receipt, please.

Potrɛbbe far seguire le mie lɛttere a quest'indirizzo?
Could you forward my letters to this address?

Sì, signore; perɔ̀ ɛ̀ necessario che riɛmpia[5] questo mɔdulo.
Yes, sir; but you'll have to fill out this form.

Tante grazie.
Many thanks.

NƆTE

1.   **uffi̇cio postale** *m.* = **pɔsta**; **pɔsta** also means *mail*; **direttore della pɔsta** *m.*, *postmaster*; **postino** or **portalɛttere** *m. letter carrier, mailman*; **vaglia (postale)** *m., money order*; **pacco postale,** *parcel post*; **casɛlla postale,** *post office box*.

2.   **mɛtterci,** *to take* (of time, with a definite subject): **il trɛno ci mette ci̇nque ore,** *the train takes five hours.* Otherwise, *to take* (of time) is expressed by **volerci: ci vuɔle un'ora,** *it takes an hour.*

[5] Present subjunctive **of riempire** (= **riɛmpiere**), *to fill, fill out.* § 49.

Dal mɛdico

At the Doctor's (Office)

Vuɔle chiamarmi un dottore? Non mi sɛnto bɛne. Sono malato (-a).

> *Will you call a doctor for me? I'm not feeling well. I'm sick.*

Cɛrto. Vuɔle uno specialista?

> *Certainly. Do you want a specialist?*

Non è necessario. Un mɛdico qualunque, ma uno che parli[1] inglese, se è possibile.

> *That isn't necessary. Any doctor, but one that speaks English, if that is possible.*

(Al telɛfono) C'è il dottor Fusco?

> (*At the telephone*) *Is Dr. Fusco in?*

(Rispondɛndo) Sono io.

> (*Replying*) *This is he.*

Potrɛbbe venire a Via Cairoli numero 61? C'è una persona che non sta bɛne.

> *Could you come to 61 Cairoli Street? There's a sick person here* (*lit. "who is not well"*).

In questo momento dɛvo andare all'ospedale ma mi fermerò un minuto a vedere il malato.

> *Right now I have to go to the hospital, but I'll stop by for a minute to see the patient.*

---

[1] **parli**, subjunctive. § 51*a*.

Grazie. . . . Non tarderà ad arrivare, signore (-a). Sarà qui
da un momento all'altro.

> *Thank you. . . . He'll be here soon, sir (madam). He'll be
> here any moment.*

Grazie. Quando arriva, mi avvisi per piacere.
(Pɔco dopo) Buɔn giorno, dottore.

> *Thank you. When he comes, please let me know.
> (A little later) How do you do, doctor.*

Che cɔsa si sɛnte?

> *What seems to be wrong?*

Mi duɔle[2] qui, ma da che Lɛi è entrato il dolore è diminuito,
dottore.

> *I have a pain here; but since you came in, doctor, the pain
> is less sharp (lit. "lessened").*

A vɔlte succɛde. Lɛi dovrɛbbe farsi fare una visita complɛta.
Può venire all'ospedale lɔ settimana prɔssima?

> *That sometimes happens. You should have a complete
> examination. Can you come to the hospital next week?*

Sì, dottore, se è necessario.

> *Yes, doctor, if it's necessary.*

Nel frattɛmpo Le scrivo una ricɛtta. C'è una nuɔva medicina
che Le calmerà il dolore.

> *Meanwhile, I'll write you a prescription. There is a new
> medicine that will stop your pain.*

C'è una farmacia in questo quartiɛre?

> *Is there a pharmacy in this neighborhood?*

Ce n'è[3] una qui sotto in piazza che sta apɛrta tutta la nɔtte.

> *There's one below in the square which stays open all night.*

NɔTE

    1. **mɛdico** = **dottore** *m.*; **gabinetto (del mɛdico)**, *office*;
ore di consultazione, *office hours*.

[2] From **dolere**. § 75 (12).   [3] §§ 38, 36.

2. Other vocabulary: **ambulanza** or **auto-ambulanza** *f.*, *ambulance*; **rimettere un ɔsso**, *to set a bone*; **attacco cardíaco**, *heart attack*; **malattia (leggiɛra, grave, crɔnica, acuta, contagiosa)**, *sickness* (*light, serious, chronic, acute, contagious*); **avere un raffreddore (di pɛtto, di tɛsta)**, *to have a cold* (*in the chest, in the head*); **infermiɛra**, *nurse*; **stare a (in) diɛta**, *to be on a diet*; **micrɔbio**, *germ*; **pressione arteriosa elevata** *f.*, *high blood pressure*; **polmonite** *f.*, *pneumonia*; **pasticche per la tosse**, *cough drops*.

Dal dentista

At the Dentist's

Buɔn giorno, signorina. Sono venuta per fissare un'ora per una consultazione.

> *Good morning, (Miss). I've come to make an appointment for a consultation.*

Subito, se vuɔle. In questo momento il dottore non è occupato. Vɛnga.

> *Immediately, if you want. Right now the doctor is not busy. Come (this way).*

Grazie. (Al dentista) Hɔ un dɛnte cariato che mi fa soffrire molto. Non pɔsso nemmeno masticare.

> *Thank you. (To the dentist) I have a cavity (lit. "decayed tooth") that gives me a great deal of pain. I can't even chew.*

Vediamo. Piɛghi la tɛsta indiɛtro e apra bɛne la bocca.

> *Let's see. Put your head back and open your mouth wide.*

Ɛ questo che mi fa male. Il dolore mi fa impazzire.

> *This is the one that hurts. The pain is driving me crazy.*

In questo dɛnte non ci vedo carie. Ah, sì, ma è un buco piccolissimo.

> *I don't see any cavity in this tooth. Oh, yes, but it's a very small cavity.*

Allora non dovrà cavarmi[1] il dɛnte?

> *Then you won't have to take the tooth out?*

---

[1] **cavare**, *to pull, take out* = **estrarre**.

Nɔ davvero! Glielo otturerɔ.[2] Non Le farɔ punto[3] male.
No, indeed! I'll fill it. I won't hurt you at all.

Meglio così. Sono molto nervosa.
That's good (lit. "better thus"). I'm very nervous.

Vuɔle un'otturazione di porcellana, d'ɔro o d'argɛnto?
Do you want a porcelain, gold or silver filling?

Di quello che a Lɛi sembri[4] più indicato. Non vorrɛi che
l'otturazione cadesse[5] dopo pɔchi giorni.
*Whatever you think best. I wouldn't want the filling to fall
out after a few days.*

Non si preɔccupi. Le durerà diɛci anni. E ora Le anestetizzo
la gengiva e non sentirà nessun dolore.
*Don't worry. It'll last ten years. And now I'll anesthesize
your gum and you won't feel any pain.*

(Più tardi) Ɛcco fatto, signorina.
(Later) There you are.

Dɛvo ritornare fra qualche giorno per un contrɔllo?
Should I come back in a few days for you to check it?

Non ɛ necessario. Buɔn giorno.
That won't be necessary. Good-bye.

Buɔn giorno.
Good-bye.

NOTE

dal dentista, *in the dentist's office* = **nel gabinetto del
dentista**; **ore di consultazione,** *office hours.*

---

[2] **otturare,** *to fill* (a tooth) = **riempire.** [3] **punto,** *at all* = **affatto.**
[4] Subjunctive. § 52. [5] Past subjunctive of **cadere.** §§ 48*a*, 54.

In farmacia

At the Drugstore

La signora des*i*dera?
> *What can I do for you (lit. "the lady wishes")?*

Una bottiglietta[1] d'aspirina per il mal di tɛsta.[2]
> *A small bottle of aspirin for a headache*

Va bɛne così?
> *Will this one do (lit. "is it all right this way")?*

Nɔ. Mi dia una bottiglietta un pɔ' più grande . . . come quella.
> *No. Give me a larger bottle . . . like that one.*

Altro?
> *Anything else?*

Sì. Delle pasticche[3] per la tosse.
> *Yes. Some coughdrops.*

Queste sono molto efficaci.
> *These are very good.*

Sono amare?
> *Are they bitter?*

Nɔ, sono dolci. Pi*a*cciono[4] anche ai bambini.
> *No, they're sweet. Even children like them.*

Vorrɛi anche uno spazzolino da dɛnti, ma non trɔppo duro.
> *I would like also a toothbrush, but not too hard.*

---

[1] **bottiglietta** and **tubetto** are diminutives of **bottiglia** and **tubo** respectively. §17*b*.
[2] **mal di tɛsta = dolor di tɛsta** *m.*   [3] **pasticche** or **past*i*glie.**   [4] § 61.

Guardi, questo è eccellɛnte.
Here, this one is excellent.

Benίssimo.   E pɔi mi occorre[5] un tubetto[1] di pasta dentifrίcia.
Fine.   And then I need a small tube of toothpaste.

Questa è la marca più popolare in Itɑlia.
This is the most popular brand in Italy.

Benίssimo.   Quanto Le dɛvo?
O.K.   How much do I owe you?

Ɛcco signora.   Paghi[6] alla cassa.
Here (madam).   Pay the cashier.

NɔTE

1.   The Italian **farmacia** is in general a true pharmacy and does not sell the sundry items one finds in the American drugstore.

2.   Other useful vocabulary in addition to **tosse**: **raffreddore** *m.*, *cold*; **avere un raffreddore (di pɛtto, di tɛsta)**, *to have a cold (in the chest, in the head)*; also **ɛssere raffreddato**, *to have a cold.*

3.   Besides meaning *to have to*, *must*, **dovere** also means *to owe.*

[5] **mi occorre** or **hɔ bisogno di,** *I need* from **occorrere** and **avere bisogno (di).**
[6] § 73.

5

Il viaggio finisce

The Trip Ends

Ferragosto

Ferragosto

Ha deciso[1] di andare a Venezia?
Did you decide to go to Venice?

Sì; vorrei partire il 15 (quindici) agosto.
Yes; I'd like to leave on the fifteenth of August.

Io Le consiglio di non partire prima del 20 (venti) o del 21 (ventuno).
I'd advise you not to leave before the twentieth or twenty-first.

Perchè?
Why?

Perchè il 15 è Ferragosto.
Because the fifteenth is Ferragosto.

È vero! Ma che cosa significa "Ferragosto?"
That's right! But what does "Ferragosto" mean?

La parola deriva dal latino e vuol dire[2] le "ferie d'agosto."
The word comes from Latin and means "the holidays of August."

---

[1] Past participle of **decidere,** *to decide.* [2] From **volere dire** = **significare.**

Sɔ che tutti fanno fɛsta quɑ in Itɑlia.

> *I know that everybody takes time off here in Italy.*

Sì. Tutti vanno[3] in vacanza e i trɛni sono affollatɪssimi.[4]

> *Yes. Everybody goes on vacation and the trains are very crowded.*

Dɛv' ɛssere una vɛcchia uɕanza.

> *It must be an old custom.*

Ɛ̀ prɔprio così. In agosto fa caldo[5] in Itɑlia, e le persone che hanno lavorato tutto l'anno hanno biɕogno di ripɔɕo.

> *That's right. In August it's very warm in Italy, and the people who have worked the whole year need a rest.*

Dove vanno in vacanza?

> *Where do they go on their vacation?*

Generalmente o in montagna o al mare: c'ɛ̀ un ɛɕodo generale dalle città.[6]

> *Usually to the mountains or to the seaside: there's a general exodus from the cities.*

M'immɑgino che le strade saranno[7] piɛne di mɑcchine.

> *I suppose that the highways are full of cars.*

Eccome. E in montagna e al mare gli albɛrghi[8] sono al complɛto.

> *You can say that again. And in the mountains and at the beaches the hotels are full.*

In tal caso rimanderɔ̀ la partɛnza per qualche[9] giorno.

> *In that case I'll put off leaving for a few days.*

NɔTE

Names of languages are masculine and are preceded by the definite article. §1*e*.

[3] § 75 (1). [4] § 24. [5] § 67. [6] § 7*d*. [7] § 45*d*. [8] § 12*a*. [9] § 19*b*.

Il viaggio a Venɛzia

The Trip to Venice

Va a Venɛzia anche Lɛi, signore?
Are you going to Venice too, (sir)?

Sì. Vɔglio vedere in tutti i mɔdi[1] la Regina dell'Adriɑtico.
Yes. I absolutely have to see the Queen of the Adriatic.

Mi dirà che io sono trɔppo curioso, ma ɛ̀ americano Lɛi?
*I hope you won't think (lit. "you'll say") that I'm too
curious, but are you an American?*

Sì. Mi trɔvo in Itɑlia da[2] circa un mese.
Yes. I've been in Italy for about a month.

Si tratterrà[3] a lungo a Venɛzia?
Are you staying (lit. "will you stay") in Venice very long?

Sfortunatamente nɔ. Fra due settimane dovrɔ̀ ripartire per
gli Stati Uniti.
*Unfortunately no. In two weeks I have to (lit. "I will have
to") leave for the United States.*

Le piace l'Itɑlia?
Do you like Italy?

Molto. Ci sono tante cɔse da vedere!
Very much. There are so many things to see.

Il trɛno rallɛnta. Arriviamo a Mɛstre.
The train's slowing down. We're reaching Mestre.

---

[1] **in tutti i mɔdi**=**in ogni mɔdo**=**ad ogni cɔsto.**   [2] § 62*a.*   [3] From **trattenersi,** *to
stay, linger,* which is conjugated like **tenere.** §§ 75 (34), 74.

Allora siamo vicini a Venɛzia.

> *Then we're near Venice.*

Sì. Fra pɔchi minuti passeremo sopra il lungo viadotto che unisce Venɛzia con la terraferma.[4]

> *Yes. In a few minutes we'll pass over the long viaduct that joins Venice with the mainland.*

(Più tardi) Ɛccoci arrivati. Quante gɔndole, quanti motoscafi e quanti canali!

> *(Later) Here we are. What a lot of gondolas, motorboats, and canals!*

Quello ɛ il Canal Grande.

> *That's the Grand Canal.*

Stasera mi riposerɔ, ma domani visiterɔ la Basílica di San Marco.

> *This evening I'll rest, but tomorrow I'll visit St. Mark's Church.*

Non dimentichi di visitare anche il Palazzo Ducale.

> *Don't forget to visit the Doges' Palace also.*

Non dubiti. Hɔ comprato una guida di Venɛzia, e vɔglio visitare tutti i posti importanti.

> *Don't worry. I've bought a guide of Venice, and I want to visit all the main places.*

NOTE

1. Some regions of Italy are: **settentrionale,** *northern* = **del nɔrd**; **meridionale,** *southern* = **del sud**; **centrale,** *central*. The cardinal points are: **nɔrd** *m.* or **settentrione** *m.*, *north*; **sud** *m.* or **mezzogiorno,** *south*; **ɛst** *m.* or **oriɛnte** *m.* or **levante** *m.*, *east*; **ɔvest** *m.* or **ponɛnte** *m.* or **occidɛnte** *m.*, *west*.

2. Some other terrain: **monte** *m.*, *mountain*; **pianura,** *plain*; **collina**, hill.

---

[4] **terraferma** = **continɛnte** *m.*

Al Lido

At the Lido

■ **Due ragazze**   *Two Girls*

Ɔggi è una giornata ideale per andare al Lido.
Today's a perfect day to go to the Lido.

È vero. Fa caldo e non tira vεnto.
It really is. It's warm and there's no wind.

Ci andiamo in gondola?
Are we going in a gondola?

Nɔ, è mεglio andarci in vaporetto. Si fa più prεsto.
No, it's better to go in a ferryboat (lit. "little steamer").
It's much quicker.

(Più tardi) Quanta gεnte, e quante cabine!
(Later) What a lot of people and what a lot of cabanas!

Come sai, il Lido di Venεzia è una delle spiagge più popolari
d'Italia.
(As) you know, the Lido of Venice is one of the most popular
beaches in Italy.

Che cɔsa è quel grand' edifìcio?
What's that big building?

Quello è l'Hotεl Excεlsior. Vi andremo più tardi.
That's the Hotel Excelsior. We'll go there later.

Ora andiamo a metterci[1] il costume da bagno.
Now let's go and put on our bathing suits.

---

[1] **mεttersi**=**indossare**.

Io non hɔ mai nuotato nel mare.
> *I've never swum in the sea.*

Vedrai che è più facile che nell'acqua dolce.
> *You'll find that it's easier than in fresh water.*

Sarà. Ma non mi piace nuotare se non pɔsso toccare il fondo.
> *That may be. But I don't like to swim if I can't touch bottom.*

(Entrando in acqua) L'acqua non è punto fredda.
> *(Going into the water) The water isn't at all cold.*

Ed è calmissima. Non c'è nemmeno un cavallone.
> *And it's very calm. There isn't even a breaker.*

Allora perchè non ti tuffi?
> *Then why don't you plunge in?*

Prima vɔglio sdraiarmi sulla sabbia, al sole.
> *First I want to stretch out on the sand, in the sun.*

Attenzione a non bruciarti!
> *Watch you don't burn yourself!*

Hai ragione. Il sole è molto fɔrte. C'è caso di prɛndere un'insolazione.[2]
> *You're right. The sun is very strong. You might get a sunstroke.*

Io faccio una nuotata.
> *I'm going to take a swim.*

Vai pure. Fra pɔchi minuti verrɔ in acqua anch'io.
> *Go ahead. In a few minutes I'm coming in the water too.*

■ **Due ragazzi**   *Two Boys*

Questa spiaggia è veramente bɛlla.
> *This beach is really beautiful.*

---

[2] **insolazione** *f.* = **colpo di sole.**

Sì. La sabbia è bianca e il mare è azzurro.
> *Yes. The sand is white and the sea is blue.*

Non ho mai[3] veduto tante cabine e tanti ombrelloni.
> *I have never seen so many cabanas and so many beach umbrellas.*

C'è molta gente oggi perchè fa caldo.[4]
> *There are a lot of people today because it's hot.*

Dove andiamo a metterci le mutandine[5] da[6] bagno?
> *Where do we go to put on our bathing trunks?*

Dovremo affittare una cabina per la giornata.
> *We'll have to rent a cabana for the day.*

Oggi il sole scotta; dovremo fare attenzione perchè non siamo ancora abbronzati.[7]
> *The sun's scorching today; we'll have to be careful because we don't have a tan yet.*

Tu sai[8] nuotare?
> *Do you know how to swim?*

Sì, ma non molto bene. È per questo che preferisco nuotare con le pinne.
> *Yes, but not very well. That's why I prefer to swim with fins.*

A me piace lo sci d'acqua e la pesca subacquea.
> *I like water skiing and spear fishing (lit. "underwater fishing").*

Perchè non affittiamo una barca? Il mare è così calmo.
> *Why don't we rent a boat? The sea is so calm.*

Perchè no!
> *Why not*

Andiamo a domandare a quel bagnino dove si affitta[9] una barca.
> *Let's go ask that lifeguard where we can rent a boat.*

---

[3] § 32b.   [4] § 67b.   [5] § 60c.   [6] § 62c.   [7] **abbronzarsi = prendere la tintarella,** *to tan, to get a tan.*   [8] § 75 (28).   [9] § 59b.

Credo che dovremo andare allo stabilimento balneare laggiù.

I think we'll have to go down there to the bath house.

Hanno un bar nello stabilimento balneare?

Do they have a café at the bath house?

Sì, sì. C'è un bar e c'è anche un ristorante.

Yes, of course. They have a café and also a restaurant.

Allora, prima di andare in barca potremo prendere una bibita fredda o un gelato.

Then before going out on the boat we'll be able to have a cold (soft) drink or an ice cream.

Ottima[10] idea!

That's a great idea.

NOTE

1.   The word **lido** = **spiaggia**, *beach*; but **Lido** is generally restricted to the beach at Venice.

2.   As well as cabanas, one may find a *bathhouse*, **stabilimento di bagni**.

3.   Other swimwear: **accappatoio**, *bathrobe*; **mutandine da bagno** *f. pl.*, *trunks*; **cuffia da nuoto** (or **di gomma**), *bathing cap.*

4.   Other vocabulary: **nuotare**, *to swim*; **il nuoto**, (the art of) *swimming*; **maestro di nuoto**, *swimming instructor*; **mantenersi a galla** = **fare il morto** (*to pretend to be dead*) = **galleggiare**, *to float*; **salvagente** *m.*, *lifesaver*; **gabbiano**, *seagull*; **trampolino**, *diving board.*

5.   **onda**, *wave.*

6.   Compare: **fare una passeggiata**, *to take a walk*; **fare una fumata**, *to have a smoke*, etc.

[10] § 24*a.*

7. **sapere** means *to know how* (*to do something*), whereas **conoscere** means *to know a person or something*: **conosco suo padre** (**Roma**), *I know his father* (*Rome*); **so scrivere a macchina**, *I know how to type.*

8. Some additional vocabulary: **maschera subacquea**, *underwater mask*; **arpione** *m.*, *harpoon.*

9. After a preposition, as in **prima di andare**, Italian takes the infinitive instead of the gerund as in English.

Il cinema

The Movies

Si va al cinema stasera?
Shall we go to the movies tonight?

Andiamo. Arriveremo a tɛmpo?
Let's go. Will we get there on time?

Credo di sì. L'ultima rappresentazione comincia alle ventuno.
I think so. The last show begins at nine.

Allora andiamo. Ma scegliamone uno che abbia[1] l'aria condizionata.
Let's go, then. But let's choose one that is airconditioned.

Ɛ una buɔn'idɛa. Fa un caldo cane.
That's a good idea. It's terribly hot (lit. "it's a dog heat").

Vediamo nel giornale quello che danno.
Let's find out from the paper what's showing.

Al Volturno danno «La suɔcera simpatica». Ɛ una pellicola[2] parlata in inglese con sottotitoli in italiano.
At the Volturno they're showing "The Congenial Mother-in-law." It's a picture (spoken) in English with Italian subtitles.

Che altro c'ɛ? Io preferisco una pellicola italiana.
What else is there? I prefer an Italian picture.

---

[1] Present subjunctive of **avere**. § 51a.   [2] **pellicola** = **film** *m.*

All'Orfɛo danno «La deviazione». Hɔ sentito dire che è una bellɨssima pellɨcola.

> *At the Orpheum they're showing "The Detour." I heard it's a very beautiful picture.*

Andiamo all'Orfɛo allora.

> *Then let's go to the Orpheum.*

Prendiamo un tassì per non arrivare tardi.

> *Let's take a taxi so as not to get there late.*

(Allo sportɛllo dei biglietti) Due biglietti d'ingrɛsso.

> (*At the ticket office*) *Two tickets.*

(Pestando il piɛde a una signora) Scuɨi. Non ci si vede affatto.

> (*Stepping on a lady's foot*) *Excuse me. You can't see a thing here.*

Arriviamo prɔprio in tɛmpo per vedere il princɨpio.

> *We're just in time to see the beginning.*

(Uscɛndo) Ti è piaciuto il programma?

> (*On leaving*) *Did you like the program?*

Molto. Ora hɔ vɔglia di fumare una sigaretta, ma hɔ dimenticato le mie a casa.

> *Very much. Now I'd like to smoke a cigarette but I left (lit. "forgot") mine at home.*

Ɛcco le mie.

> *I've got mine (lit. "here are mine").*

NƆTE

1. The opposite of **credo di sì** is **credo di nɔ**.

2. An alternative expression: **sono in un bagno di sudore**, *I'm perspiring all over* (lit. "I'm in a bath of perspiration").

3. Another kind of film: **disegni animati** *m. pl.*, *cartoon*.

4. **Vedere**, *to see*; **vederci**, *to be able to see*; **non lo vedo**, *I don't see him*; **non ci vedo**, **è trɔppo buio**, *I can't see, it's too dark*.

L'esposizione di pitture

The Painting Exhibition

Mi saprebbe dire dov'è l'esposizione di pitture?
Could you tell me where the painting exhibition is?

Sì, signore. Ci vado anch'io. Se vuole, possiamo andarci insieme.
Yes, (sir). I'm going there, too. If you like, we can go together.

Con molto piacere. Siccome io sono straniero (-a), non conosco queste vie.
With pleasure. As I'm a foreigner, I'm not acquainted with these streets.

Siamo già arrivati. Questa è l'entrata.
Well, here we are (lit. "we have already arrived"). This is the entrance.

Guardi quel paesaggio a olio. È una composizione bellissima.
Look at that landscape in oils. It's a very beautiful composition.

A me piace di più questo quadro¹ impressionistico.
I prefer this impressionistic painting.

Davvero? Ma gli manca la tecnica. È mal disegnato² e peggio dipinto.³
Really? But it lacks technique. The drawing is bad and the painting is worse (lit. "it is badly drawn and worse painted").

¹ **quadro**=**pittura**. ² **disegno**, *drawing*. ³ Irregular past participle of **dipingere** (=**pitturare**), *to paint.*

Non è bello secondo l'arte classica, tuttavia c'è emozione, calore, vita.

It's not beautiful according to classic art, but it has emotion, warmth, life.

Io preferisco l'arte dei classici, che è di tutti i tempi.

I prefer classic art (lit. "of the classics") which is timeless.

Ma quella è un'arte fredda. Esprime solamente la realtà esteriore, ciò che vedono gli occhi.

But it's a cold art. It expresses only outer reality, what the eyes see.

E i moderni non vedono con gli occhi?

And don't the moderns see with their eyes?

Sì, ma vanno più in là, vanno all'anima delle cose senza mettere dettagli inutili.

Yes, but they go beyond that; they go to the soul of things, without putting in useless details.

Però mancano di logica e di buon gusto.

But they lack logic and good taste.

Vediamo il quadro su questo cavalletto.

Let's look at the painting on this easel.

Guardi questo quadro a olio, signora. Come Le pare?

Look at this oil painting, madam. How do you like it?

Per quanto lo vende?

How much are you selling it for?

Centomila lire. È una vera occasione.

One hundred thousand lire. It's a real bargain.

Le do diecimila lire.

I'll give you ten thousand lire.

Grazie. Non sto ancora morendo[4] di fame.

Thanks. I'm not starving to death yet.

[4] § 57.

Va bɛne . . . aspetterò
O.K. . . . I'll wait.

Le piace il quadro che è su questo cavalletto?
Do you like the painting that's on this easel?

Moltissimo. Mi fa venire l'acquolina in bocca.
Very much. It makes my mouth water.

Che dice? Che Le fa venire l'acquolina in bocca un tramonto?
What (lit. "what do you say")? (That) a sunset makes your mouth water?

Cotesto è un tramonto?
Is that a sunset?

Ma è chiaro!
Why of course!

Io, invece, credevo che fosse[5] un uɔvo fritto.
But I thought it was a fried egg.

Si vede che Lɛi ha fame.
Evidently (lit. "one sees that") you're hungry.

Questo però m'incanta. I colori di quegli avvoltoi sono magnifici. Che espressione ferɔce nei loro ɔcchi! Lɛi non dovrɛbbe dipingere che avvoltoi!
But I love this one. The coloring of those vultures is magnificent. What a ferocious expression in their eyes! You should be painting nothing but vultures!

Ma non sono mica[6] avvoltoi! Sono angeli!
But they're not vultures at all! They're angels.

Ɔggi non ne azzecco prɔprio una!
I just can't hit the nail on the head today!

NƆTE

1. **pittura ad ɔlio (ad acquerɛllo, a pastɛllo),** *oil (water color, pastel) painting;* **affresco,** *fresco;* **mosaico,** *mosaic.*

2. **di più = più. Di più** is used instead of **più** at the end of a sentence: **quando mangio a casa mangio di più,** *when I eat at home I eat more.*

[5] Past subjunctive of **ɛssere.** §§ 48a, 54.   [6] Reinforced negative.

Il teatro dell'ɔpera

The Opera House

(Allo sportɛllo) Ha ancora qualche biglietto per l'ɔpera di stasera?

> (*At the ticket office*) *Do you have any more tickets for tonight's opera?*

(Il venditore di biglietti) Sono quasi esauriti. Tutti li comprano anticipatamente.

> (*The ticket seller*) *They're almost all sold out. Everyone buys them in advance.*

E così non tardano a finire, vero?

> *And so they're soon gone, aren't they?*

Ɛh, già! Lɛi sa bɛne che la domenica i teatri sono sɛmpre gremiti.[1]

> *That's right! You know that on Sunday the theaters are always filled.*

Volevo due poltrone.

> *I wanted two orchestra seats.*

Di nɔna o di dɛcima[2] fila?

> *In the ninth or tenth row?*

Di dɛcima. Quanto cɔstano?

> *In the tenth. How much are they?*

Ventimila lire per tutti e due.

> *Twenty thousand lire for the pair.*

Non volevo spɛndere tanto.

> *I didn't want to spend that much.*

---

[1] **gremito = affollato.**   [2] § 77.

Allora vuɔle due posti di galleria di prima fila?

Then do you want two first-row balcony seats?

Sì, grazie.

Yes, thank you.

Di lì si vede bɛne e non è necessario venire in smoking.

From there you can see well and you don't need to wear a tuxedo.

A che ora comincia l'ɔpera?

What time does the opera begin?

Alle 21 (ventuno) in punto.

Nine sharp.

Mi dica, quando tɛrmina la stagione lirica?

Tell me, when does the opera season end?

Terminerà tra una settimana con una serata di gala.

It will close one week from today with a gala performance.

Hɔ avuto la fortuna di arrivare prima che finisca.[3]

I've been lucky to get here before it ends.

Questo programma indica tutte le rappresentazioni e la distribuzione delle parti per questa settimana.

This program shows all the performances and the casts for this week.

Guarda (guardi)[4] quante signore scollate e quanti uɔmini in smoking.

Look at all the women in their low-cut gowns and all the men in black tie (lit. "tuxedo").

Quelli vanno a occupare le poltrone e i palchi.

They'll sit in the orchestra seats and in the loges (or boxes).

Ɛcco la maschera.[5]

Here's the usher.

---

[3] Subjunctive. § 50*b*.   [4] The verbs in parentheses (**guardi,** *etc.*) are the corresponding polite counterparts of the given familiar forms.   [5] **maschera** = **inserviɛnte** *m.* and *f.*

Non ti dimenticare (non si dimentichi) di chiedere il programma.

Don't forget to ask for a program.

(Già seduti) Non so se quest'opera ti (Le) piacerà.

(Seated) I don't know whether you'll like this opera.

E perchè no? Mi hanno detto che la musica è divina.

(And) why not? I've been told that the music is beautiful.

Prendi (prenda) questo binocolo e guarda (guardi) se vedi (vede) qualche amico. Il teatro è pieno.

Take these opera glasses and see if you can find any of our friends. The house is packed.

L'orchestra ha incominciato a suonare e si alza il sipario.

The orchestra has begun playing and the curtain is rising.

Si sente il suggeritore. Ma che tossire è questo!

You can hear the prompter. And I can't believe the coughing (lit. "what a coughing is this").

Pare che il pubblico si sia raffreddato apposta.

It seems as if the audience has caught cold on purpose.

(Dopo il primo atto) Che applausi!

(After the first act) What applause!

Sono già sei volte che chiamano i cantanti alla ribalta.

The singers have had six curtain calls already.

Il tenore ha cantato straordinariamente bene.

The tenor sang extraordinarily well.

Ha molta voce ed è un grand'artista.

He has a big voice and is a great artist.

Il soprano, però, non ha molta scuola. Ogni tanto stona.

But the soprano lacks training. Every once in a while she sings off key.

Ha più bocca che voce.

Her mouth is bigger than her voice.

Il bar*i*tono, invece, ha una voce molto melodiosa.
The baritone, on the other hand, has a very melodious voice.

Zitto (-a). Ɛcco il direttore.
Quiet. There's the conductor.

NƆTE

1. The whole downstairs of a theater is called **platɛa**; **palco**, *box*; **camerino**, *dressing room*; **quinte**, *wings*; **suggeritore** *m.*, *prompter.*

2. Other dress: **marsina** or **frac** *m*,. *dress coat, cutaway.*

3. Other vocabulary to do with the voice: **basso**, *bass*; **bar*i*tono**, *baritone*; **voce fɔrte** (or **potɛnte**) *f.*, *strong voice*; **nɔta di pɛtto**, *chest note.*

4. **stɔna** also suggests: **ɛssere scordato**, *to be out of tune* (instrument): **il pianofɔrte ɛ̀ scordato**, *the piano is out of tune*; **l'accordatore non l'ha accordato**, *the tuner has not tuned it.*

Natale

Christmas

È festeggiato come in America il Natale in Italia?
Is Christmas celebrated in Italy the way it is in America?

Da quello che ho sentito dire, in Italia non festeggiamo il Natale con tanto splendore come nel Suo paese.
From what I've heard, in Italy we don't make such an occasion of Christmas as in your country (lit. "we don't celebrate Christmas . . . with so much splendor").

Noi Americani consideriamo il Natale la più grande festa dell'anno.
We Americans consider Christmas the biggest holiday of the year.

Da noi[1] il Natale è soprattutto una festa religiosa.
With us Christmas is mainly a religious celebration.

In America i negozi fanno affari d'oro durante il mese di Dicembre.
In America the stores do an enormous business (lit. "business of gold") during the month of December.

Perchè?
Why?

Perchè tutti gli Americani si scambiano regali e cartoline di Natale.
Because all Americans exchange gifts and Christmas cards.

Noi, invece, mandiamo soltanto qualche cartolina di Natale.
We, on the other hand, send only a few Christmas cards.

---

[1] § 62e.

Ma almeno non avete gli alberi di Natale?
> *But don't you at least have Christmas trees?*

Solamente nelle grandi città. Nei piccoli paesi in generale i bambini italiani ricevono alcuni doni il sei gennaio.
> *Only in the big cities. In the small towns in general Italian children receive a few presents on the sixth of January.*

E perchè il sei gennaio?
> *And why on the sixth of January?*

Perchè quello è il giorno dell'Epifania, o come si dice più comunemente, della Befana.
> *Because that is Epiphany, or, as it is more commonly called, the Befana's day.*

Chi è la Befana?
> *Who is the Befana?*

È una grossa vecchia molto buona, che entra nelle case pei camini e porta regali ai bambini.
> *She's a big, very kind, old woman who gets into houses through the chimneys and brings gifts to the children.*

Proprio come il Santa Claus dei bambini americani.
> *Just like the American children's Santa Claus.*

Mi dica, in Italia non si fa[2] nulla di speciale a Natale?
> (*Tell me*), *don't they do anything special in Italy at Christmas?*

Certo. Specialmente nelle grandi città quasi tutti vanno a visitare una o più chiese.
> *Certainly. Especially in the big cities almost everyone goes to visit one or more churches.*

Perchè?
> *Why?*

Per vedere il Presepio.
> *To see the Presepio (lit. "crib," "manger").*

[2] § 59b.

Che cos'è il Presepio?

What's the Presepio?

È la rappresentazione della nascita di Gesù.

It's the representation of the birth of Jesus.

È una specie di spettacolo teatrale?

Is it a kind of theatrical performance?

No, no! In una parte della chiesa costruiscono una specie di grotta, come quella di Betlemme, e dentro vi³ mettono un Bambino Gesù, la Vergine Maria, San⁴ Giuseppe, i Re Magi' dei pastori, ecc.

No, no! In one part of the church a kind of grotto is constructed, like the one in Bethlehem, and a Christ Child, the Virgin Mary, Saint Joseph, the Magi Kings, shepherds, etc., are put in it.

Devono essere molto belli questi Presepi.

These Presepi must be very beautiful.

Dei veri capolavori. In alcune famiglie, poi, i ragazzi si divertono a preparare un piccolo Presepio in casa loro.

Real masterpieces. In some families the boys enjoy preparing a little Presepio in their own homes.

Mi dispiace proprio che non potrò trattenermi in Italia fino a Natale.

I'm really very sorry that I won't be able to stay in Italy until Christmas time.

Peccato davvero. In ogni modo, se Lei passerà il Natale in una grande città americana, non dimentichi⁵ di andare in un negozio italiano e di comprare un panforte o dei torroni. Sono dolci squisiti.

It's a real pity. Anyhow, if you spend Christmas in a large American city, don't forget to go to an Italian store and buy a panforte and some torroni. They're delicious sweets.

³ **vi = ci.** § 38.   ⁴ §16c.   ⁵ **dimenticare**, *to forget*; **mancare**, *to fail.* § 73a.

Non mancherò.

> *I sure will (lit. "I shall not fail").*

NOTE

1. **Buon Natale!** *Merry Christmas!* **la Vigilia di Natale,** *Christmas Eve*; **fare vigilia,** *to fast*; **Buon Capo d'Anno!** *Happy New Year!* **Pasqua,** *Easter*: **Buona (Felice) Pasqua!** *Happy Easter!* **settimana santa,** *Holy Week*; **giovedì santo,** *Holy Thursday*; **venerdì santo,** *Good Friday.*

2. **Befana,** or **Befania,** is a corruption of **Epifania,** *Epiphany.* It was on January 6 that the Wise Men visited the infant Jesus and gave him presents.

3. **Panforte** *m.* is a kind of hard, one-inch-thick fruitcake; **torrone** *m.*, is a nougat candy.

Attraverso l'Italia

Through Italy

Quali altre città dovrei visitare prima di fare ritorno negli Stati Uniti?
What other cities should I visit before returning to the United States?

Poichè deve prendere l'aereo a Milano, vada prima a Padova e a Vicenza.
Since you have to get the plane in Milan, go to Padua and Vicenza first.

Ne vale proprio la pena?
Is it really worthwhile?

Eh, sì! Padova per gli affreschi di Giotto e Vicenza per l'architettura del Palladio.
Oh, yes! Padua for Giotto's frescos, and Vicenza for Palladio's architecture.

La valle del Po è molto ricca, vero?
The Po valley is very rich, isn't it?

Sì, è una valle fertilissima.
Yes, it's a very fertile valley.

Sulle montagne vicine ci sono anche molti bei posti per gli sport invernali.[1]
On the mountains nearby there are also a lot of beautiful places for winter sports.

---

[1] inverno, *winter*, (adj.) invernale.

È vero. C'è anche Cortina d'Ampɛzzo, che è il soggiorno invernale più nɔto.

> *That's true. There's also Cortina d'Ampezzo, which is the best-known winter resort.*

Sì, sì. Nelle Alpi.

> *Yes. In the Alps.*

Le piace sciare?

> *Do you like to ski?*

Moltissimo, ma preferisco pattinare sul ghiaccio.

> *Very much, but I prefer to skate (on the ice).*

Caspita, com'è tardi! Sono le undici e quaranta. Allora, se non ci rivediamo prima della Sua partɛnza, buɔn viaggio.

> *Hey, it's late! It's twenty minutes to twelve. Well, if we don't see each other again before you leave, bon voyage!*

Grazie. Arrivederla, e buɔna nɔtte.

> *Thank you. Good-bye, and good night.*

NɔTE

1. Other seasons of the year: **primavɛra**, *spring*, (adj.) **primaverile**; **estate** *f. summer*, (adj.) **estivo**; **autunno**, *autumn*, (adj.) **autunnale**.

2. Some equipment: **sci** *m. pl.*, *skis*; **pattini** *m. pl.*, *skates*.

La visita d'addio

The Farewell Visit

Ah, signor Brown! Che piacere rivederLa!
> *Oh, John (lit. Mr. Brown)! How good it is to see you again.*

Caro signor Nardi!
> *Good to see you, Giovanni (lit. "dear Mr. Nardi")!*

Passi di qua. S'accomodi!
> *Come right this way. Sit down.*

Grazie. Ho un po' fretta.[1]
> *Thank you. I'm a little pressed for time.*

Mi è stato detto che parte domani.
> *I was told you're leaving tomorrow.*

È vero. E io sono venuto a salutarLa.
> *Right. And I've come to say good-bye (to you).*

Bravo!
> *That was nice of you (lit. "well done")!*

Non   dimenticherò mai tutte le Sue cortesie.
> *I'll never forget your kindness.*

Le pare! L'importante è che il Suo soggiorno nella nostra città sia stato piacevole.
> *Not at all. The important thing is that your stay in our city has been pleasant.*

Ne può essere certo. Venezia è un incanto!
> *You may be sure of that. Venice is a dream (lit. "an enchantment")!*

---

[1] **aver fretta** = **aver premura**.

Sì, una città meravigliosa.
> *Yes, it's a wonderful city.*

Mi sono divertito un mondo, ed hɔ imparato tante cɔse.
> *I've enjoyed myself immensely and I've learned a lot (lit. "many things").*

Mi fa piacere.
> *I'm glad of that.*

E ora tɔlgo[2] il disturbo.
> *And now I'll not trouble you any longer.*

Tutt'altro! Quando ritornerà[3] sarà il benvenuto.
> *No trouble at all. When you come back, you'll be welcome.*

Grazie mille, signor Nardi. Arrivederci.
> *Thank you very much, Giovanni (lit. Mr. Nardi). Good-bye.*

Arrivederci e buɔn viaggio.
> *Good-bye and bon voyage!*

NOTE

1.   The opposite of **di qua** is **di là**.

2.   Other expressions with **fretta**: **non c'è fretta**, *there's no hurry*; **affrettatevi** (or **si affretti**) = **fate** (or **faccia**) **prɛsto**, *hurry up*.

[2] From tɔgliere. § 75 (35).   [3] § 45*f*.

APPENDIX

1. The Definite Article *the*

	SINGULAR	PLURAL
Masc.	**il, lo, (l')**	**i, gli, (gl')**

The usual masculine forms are **il**, for the singular, and **i**, for the plural:

il treno	the train
i treni	the trains
il soldo	the penny
i soldi	the pennies

Lo and **gli** are used before masculine words beginning with **s** + consonant or with **z**. **L'** is used before a masculine word beginning with a vowel; its plural is **gli**, which may become **gl'** before an i.

lo spillo	the pin
gli spilli	the pins
lo zio	the uncle
gli zii	the uncles
l'amico	the friend
gli amici	the friends
l'Italiano	the Italian
gl'Italiani	(the) Italians

	SINGULAR	PLURAL
Fem.	la (l')	le (l')

La becomes **l'** before any vowel. **Le** may become **l'** only before **e**.

la casa	the house
le case	the houses
l'automobile	the automobile
le automobili	the automobiles
l'esposizione	the exhibition
l'esposizioni	the exhibitions

2. The definite article is used

   a) With nouns used in a general sense:

I soldati portano l'uniforme.	Soldiers wear a uniform.
Il pane è nutriente.	Bread is nourishing.

   b) With abstract nouns:

Il valore è necessario.	Courage is necessary.

   c) With names of countries, continents, states, large islands:

L'Italia è un bel paese	Italy is a beautiful country
La California è negli Stati Uniti.	California is in the United States.
La Sicilia è un'isola.	Sicily is an island.

   BUT:

Malta è vicino alla Sicilia.	Malta is near Sicily.

   With names of unmodified feminine countries the article is omitted after **in**, and sometimes after the preposition **di**:

Vado in Italia.	I am going to Italy.
Le città d'Italia.	The cities of Italy.

   BUT:

Nella Francia meridionale.	In southern France.
La storia dell'Italia antica.	The history of ancient Italy.

d) With surnames (not preceded by a given name);

Il Cellini nacque a Firɛnze.   Cellini was born in Florence.

e) With adjectives denoting names of languages:

L'italiano è melodioso.   Italian is melodious.

Except immediately after **parlare** and **in**:

Parlo francese.   I speak French.
Lo dica in inglese.   Say it in English.

f) With a title not in direct address:

Il signor Bianchi è giovane.   Mr. Bianchi is young.
Il dottor Ceri è qui.   Doctor Ceri is here.

g) With nouns of weight and measure:

Cɔsta un dɔllaro la libbra.   It costs one dollar a pound.
Vuɔle due dɔllari il mɛtro.   He wants two dollars a meter.

h) Instead of the possessive adjective with parts of the body, and articles of clothing when the meaning is clear:

Mi duɔle la mano.   My hand hurts.
Si metta il cappɛllo.   Put on your hat.

i) With names of days (modified), seasons, meals, expressions of time, etc.:

Partirɔ il lunedì prɔssimo.   I shall leave next Monday.
La primavɛra è bɛlla.   Spring is beautiful.
Il pranzo è pronto.   Dinner is ready.
Venne l'anno passato.   He came last year.
Sono le tre.   It's three o'clock.

j) Before an infinitive used as a noun when it begins a sentence:

Il viaggiare è istruttivo.   Traveling is educational.

3. The Indefinite Article *a, an*.

Masc.	**un**	**uno**
Fem.	**una**	**(un')**

The usual masculine form is **un**. **Uno** is used before a masculine word beginning with s + consonant or with **z**. **Una** becomes **un'** before a vowel.

un treno	a train
un americano	an American
uno studio	a study
uno zio	an uncle
una casa	a house
un'americana	an American woman

4. The indefinite article (**un, una, un'**) is omitted

   a) Before certain unmodified predicate nouns used as adjectives:

È soldato.	He is a soldier.
Sono italiano.	I am an Italian.

   BUT:

È un aviatore famoso.	He is a famous aviator.

   b) Before **cento, mille**:

cento (mille) uomini	a hundred (a thousand) men.

   c) After **che**, *what a*, and after certain verbs especially when negative:

Che donna!	What a woman!
Non ho automobile.	I haven't got a car.

5. Nouns are masculine or feminine. If a noun denotes a male being, it is masculine; if it denotes a female being, it is feminine.

il padre	the father
la madre	the mother
l'uomo	the man
la donna	the woman

   a) The masculine plural of certain nouns may denote both genders:

i re	the kings and queens
i miei fratelli	my brothers and sisters

6. Nouns ending

a) In **-o** are generally masculine:

il cielo   the sky
il denaro the money

EXCEPTIONS:
la mano   the hand
la radio the radio

b) In **-a** (also **-ione**) are generally feminine:

la casa   the house
la nazione the nation

Some nouns in **-ma** and **-ta** are exceptions:

il clima   the climate
il problema the problem
il poeta   the poet
il profeta the prophet

7. Plural of Nouns. In general, if a noun ends

a) In **-o**, change **-o** to **-i**:

il libro the book
i libri   the books

EXCEPTIONS:

(1) The plural of a noun ending in unstressed **-io** has only one **i**.

lo specchio   the mirror
gli specchi   the mirrors

BUT:

lo zio   the uncle
gli zii the uncles

(2) A few nouns ending in **-o** are masculine in the singular but have feminine forms in the plural:

il frutto the fruit
le frutta the fruits
il dito   the finger
le dita   the fingers

il br*a***ccio**	the arm
le br*a***ccia**	the arms
l'u*ɔ***vo**	the egg
le u*ɔ***va**	the eggs
etc.	

(3) **u***ɔ***mo**   man   **u***ɔ***mini**   men

b) In -**a**, change -**a** to -**e**:

la casa	the house
le case	the houses

EXCEPTIONS: Masculine nouns ending in -**a** change -**a** to -**i**:

il probl*ε***ma**	the problem
i probl*ε***mi**	the problems
il po*ε***ta**	the poet
i po*ε***ti**	the poets

c) In -**e**, change -**e** to -**i**:

il padre	the father
i padri	the fathers
la madre	the mother
le madri	the mothers

d) In an accented vowel or in a consonant, it is invai iable:

la città	the city
le città	the cities
il lapis	the pencil
i lapis	the pencils

e) In -**i** and -**ie**, it is also invariable:

la cri*s***i**	the depression
le cri*s***i**	the depressions
la sp*ε***cie**	the species
le sp*ε***cie**	the species

EXCEPTIONS: **la moglie** the wife   **le mogli** the wives

8. Possession is expressed by the preposition **di**, which may become **d'** before a vowel:

L'autom*ɔ***bile di Giovanni**   John's car

9. Adjectives agree in gender and in number with the nouns they modify.:

un uɔmo alto	a tall man
una dɔnna alta	a tall woman
due uɔmini alti	two tall men
due dɔnne alte	two tall women

a) An adjective modifying two nouns of different genders is generally masculine:

le mani e i piɛdi puliti   the clean hands and feet.

10. The Feminine of Adjectives

a) If the ending is -o, change -o to -a:

alto, alta	high, tall
basso, bassa	low, short

b) Otherwise there is no change:

un libro verde	a green book
una pɔrta verde	a green door

11. The Plural of Adjectives

Adjectives ending in -o, change -o to -i; those ending in -a change -a to -e; those ending in -e change -e to -i:

alto	alti	alta	alte	verde	verdi.

12. Nouns and adjectives ending in -co, and stressed on the next-to-the-last syllable, take an h in the plural in order to retain the hard sound of the singular:

parco	park
parchi	parks
bianco	white
bianchi	white

BUT:

mɛdico	doctor
mɛdici	doctors

EXCEPTIONS:

amico	friend
amici	friends
nemico	enemy
nemici	enemies
grεco	Greek
grεci	Greek
pɔrco	pig
pɔrci	pigs

a) Nouns ending in **-go** take an **h** in the plural:

cat*a*logo	catalogue.
cat*a*loghi	catalogues.

13. Nouns and adjectives ending in **-ca** and **-ga** take an **h** in the plural:

amica	friend
amiche	friends
larga	wide
larghe	wide

a) Nouns and adjectives ending in unstressed **-cia** and **-gia** drop the **i** in the plural:

val*i*gia	suitcase
valige	suitcases
m*a*ncia	tip
mance	tips

BUT:

farmacia	drugstore
farmacie	drugstores

14. Apocopation (*i.e.* dropping of the final vowel of a word before another word)

a) Words of more than one syllable ending in **-e** or **-o** preceded by **l**, **m**, **n**, or **r** frequently drop the **-e** or **-o** before another word:

si*a*m(o) pronti   we are ready

aver(e) fretta   to be in a hurry
son(o) tornati   they have come back

b) Titles ending in **-re**, such as **signore, dottore**, etc, drop the final **-e** before a name:

Il signor Doni.   Mr. Doni.
Il dottor Rossi.   Dr. Rossi.

15. Position

a) Descriptive adjectives generally follow the noun, unless the quality is inherent:

un cavallo bianco   a white horse

BUT:

la bianca neve   the white snow

b) Articles, possessive adjectives, and other common and limiting adjectives precede the noun:

molte persone   many people
un buɔn ragazzo   a good boy

c) A few adjectives change meaning according to their position:

un dɔnna pɔvera   a poor woman
una pɔvera dɔnna   an unfortunate woman
un uɔmo grande   a large man
un grand'uɔmo   a great man

d) In a question, the predicate adjective is placed before a noun subject:

Ɛ́ facile la lezione?   Is the lesson easy?

16. Irregular Adjectives. When preceding a noun

υ) **quello, bɛllo** assume forms similar to those of the definite article:

quel, quei, quello, quell', quegli, quella, quelle
bɛl, bɛi, bɛllo, bɛll', bɛgli, bɛlla, bɛlle

quel libro	that book
quei libri	those books
bɛlla dɔnna	beautiful woman
bɛlle dɔnne	beautiful women
quello spɛcchio	that mirror
quegli spɛcchi	those mirrors
bɛll'automɔbile	beautiful car
bɛlle automɔbili	beautiful cars

b) **buɔno,** in the singular, has these forms: **buɔn, buɔna, buɔn',** which are used like the indefinite article:

un buɔn libro	a good book
una buɔna ragazza	a good girl
una buɔn'insalata	a good salad

c) **grande** and **santo** become **gran** and **san** before a masculine noun beginning with a consonant, except **z** and **s** + consonant, and become **grand'** and **sant'** before any noun beginning with a vowel:

San Francesco	Saint Francis
un grande spɛcchio	a large mirror
un grand'uɔmo	a great man

17. In Italian it is possible to express several shades of meaning by adding suffixes to a noun, and even to an adjective.

a) Bigness is denoted by **-one, -ona**:

| **un ragazzone** | a big boy |
| **una ragazzona** | a big girl |

b) Smallness is denoted by **-ino** and **-etto**:

| **un ragazzino** (*or* **ragazzetto**) | a little boy |
| **una ragazzina** (*or* **ragazzetta**) | a little girl |

c) Scorn and worthlessness are denoted by *-accio*:

un ragazz*accio*   a bad boy

18. Contractions
Certain prepositions combine with the definite article as follows:

Preposition before	il	i	lo	l'	la	gli	le
a (*to, at*)	al	ai	allo	all'	alla	agli	alle
da *from, by*)	dal	dai	dallo	dall'	dalla	dagli	dalle
di (*of*)	del	dei	dello	dell'	della	degli	delle
in (*in*)	nel	nei	nello	nell'	nella	negli	nelle
su (*on*)	sul	sui	sullo	sull'	sulla	sugli	sulle

Con, *with*, and **per**, *for*, are also occasionally combined with the definite article, but it is preferable to use the separate forms.

19. The Partitive

a) The idea of *some* or *any* is frequently expressed by **di** + the definite article:

Compriamo dei fiori. We are buying some flowers.

b) Sometimes the partitive idea is expressed by **alcuni, alcune**, and also by **qualche. Alcuni** and **alcune** are plural forms.

C'ɛrano alcuni uɔmini (al- There were some men (women).
cune dɔnne).

Qualche is always followed by a singular noun:

Tutti i giorni ricevo qualche Every day I receive a few
lɛttera. letters.

c) When the sentence is negative or interrogative the partitive idea is seldom expressed in Italian:

Non hɔ comprato fiori. I haven't bought any flowers.
Lɛi riceve (delle) lɛttere? Do you receive any letters?

20. Comparison of Adjectives. Place **più**, *more*, or **meno**, *less*, before the adjective.

facile easy
più (meno) facile more (less) easy

a) Irregular:

buɔno good

migliore	better, best
cattivo	bad
peggiore	worse, worst
grande	large
maggiore	larger, older
piccolo	small
minore	smaller, younger

21. Comparison of Equality. Così ... come (also: tanto
... quanto), as (so) ... as.

così interessante come   as interesting as

22. Comparison of Inequality. Più (meno) ... di (or che),
more (less) ... than.

a) In general, than = di:

Carlo è più diligɛnte di Gio-vanni.	Charles is more diligent than John.
Carlo ha più di diɛci lire.	Charles has more than ten lire.

b) Than = che when the comparison concerns the same
subject and is made between two nouns, adjectives,
verbs or adverbs:

Mangio più pane che carne.	I eat more bread than meat.
Carlo è più diligɛnte che in-telligɛnte.	Charles is more diligent than intelligent.
Fa più freddo qui che là.	It is colder here than there.

c) Than = di quel che, or che non, before an inflected verb.

| Egli è più intelligɛnte di quel che sembra. | He is more intelligent than he seems. |

23. Other Comparisons

a) tanto, -a ... quanto   as much ... as
   tanti, -e ... quanto   as many ... as
   Hɔ tanti libri quanto lɛi.   I have as many books as she.

b) (quanto) più ... (tanto) più   the more ... the more
   (quanto) meno ... (tanto) meno   the less ... the less

Più si studia, più s'impara.   The more one studies, the
more one learns.

24. The absolute superlative in **-issimo** denotes an extreme
degree without definite comparison:

molt*i*ssimo	very much
car*i*ssimo	very dear
ben*i*ssimo	very well

a) Irregular absolute superlatives of adjectives:

bu*ɔ*no	good
*ɔ*ttimo	very good
cattivo	bad
p*ɛ*ssimo	very bad
grande	large
m*a*ssimo	very large
p*i*ccolo	small
m*i*nimo	very small

Note, however, that the regular forms: **bu*ɔ*n*i*ssimo, cat-
tiv*i*ssimo, grand*i*ssimo, piccol*i*ssimo** are also in use.

25. Possessive Adjectives

MASCULINE		FEMININE		
Singular	*Plural*	*Singular*	*Plural*	
il mio	i mi*ɛ*i	la mia	le mie	my
il tuo	i tu*ɔ*i	la tua	le tue	your *(familiar)*
il suo	i su*ɔ*i	la sua	le sue	his, her, its, your *(polite)*[1]
il n*ɔ*stro	i n*ɔ*stri	la n*ɔ*stra	le n*ɔ*stre	our
il v*ɔ*stro	i v*ɔ*stri	la v*ɔ*stra	le v*ɔ*stre	your
il loro	i loro	la loro	le loro	their, your *(polite)*

a) Possessives agree in gender and number with the thing
possessed:

Il mio capp*ɛ*llo e la mia cravatta.   My hat and my tie.

b) The definite article which precedes the Italian pos-

---

[1] With the meaning of your, **Suo, Su*ɔ*i, Sua, Sue** are sometimes written with
a capital *s*, and **Loro** with a capital *l*.

sessive adjective is omitted in direct address, and before a singular, unmodified noun denoting family relationship.

Mio caro amico . . . .   My dear friend . . .
Mio padre è vɛcchio.   My father is old.

26. To avoid confusion one may say instead of **il suo libro** (*his, her, your book*): **il libro di lui** (**lɛi, Lɛi**), *his* (*her, your*) *book*.

27. Possessive Pronouns

The forms of the possessive pronouns are identical with those of the possessive adjectives.

28. Demonstrative Adjectives

*S*INGULAR		PLURAL		
Masc.	*Fem.*	*Masc.*	*Fem.*	
questo	**questa**	**questi**	**queste**	this, these (*near speaker*)
cotesto	**cotesta**	**cotesti**	**coteste**	that, those (*near person spoken to*)
quello	**quella**	**quelli**	**quelle**	that, those (*away from both*)

The adverbs **qu***i* and **qu***a*, *here*, correspond to **questo**; **costì** and **costà**, *there*, to **cotesto**; and **lì** and **là**, *there*, to **quello**.

29. Demonstrative Pronouns

The forms of the demonstrative pronouns .are identical with those of the demonstrative adjectives. In addition we have:

a) The pronoun **ciò** which is frequently used instead of **questo, cotesto,** or **quello.**

b) Two masculine singular pronouns used only with persons: **questi**, *the latter*, and **quegli**, *the former*.

30. Adverbs of manner may be formed by adding **-mente** to the feminine singular of the adjective:

r*a*pido, -a   rapid

rapidamente   rapidly

Adjectives ending in **-le** or **-re** preceded by a vowel drop the **-e** before adding **-mente**:

facile	easy
facilmente	easily
regolare	regular
regolarmente	regularly

EXCEPTIONS:

buɔno	good
bɛne	well
cattivo	bad
male	badly

31. Comparison of adverbs is the same as for adjectives (*see* § 20).

bɛne	well
mɛglio	better, best
ottimamente	very well
male	badly
pɛggio	worse, worst
pessimamente	very badly
pɔco	little
meno	less, least
poch*i*ssimo	very little
molto	much
più	more, most
molt*i*ssimo	very much

32. Negatives

a) **Non**, *not*, is placed before the verb:

Vedo.	I see.
Non vedo.	I do not see.

b) If negative words are used after the verb, **non** must precede:

Non vedo niɛnte.	I see nothing.
Non canto mai.	I never sing.

BUT:

Niɛnte vedo.	I see nothing.
Mai canto.	I never sing.

33. Personal Pronouns

PER-SON		SUBJECT	DIRECT OBJECT	INDIRECT OBJECT	REFLEXIVE	OBJECT OF A PREPOSITION
SINGULAR	1	io I	mi me	mi to me	mi myself	(per) me
	2	tu you (*familiar*)	ti you	ti to you	ti yourself	(per) te
	3	egli (esso) he, (it)	lo him, (it)	gli to him (to it)	si himself, (itself)	(per) lui (esso)
		ella (essa) she, (it)	la her, (it)	le to her, (to it)	si herself, (itself)	(per) lɛi (essa)
		Lɛi you (*polite*)	La you	Le to you	si yourself	(per) Lɛi
PLURAL	1	noi we	ci us	ci to us	ci ourselves	(per) noi
	2	voi you (*semiformal when addressing one person*)	vi you	vi to you	vi yourself, yourselves	(per) voi
	3	essi, esse they	li (*m.*), le (*f.*) them	loro to them	si themselves	(per) loro (essi, esse)
		Loro you	Li you (*m.*) Le you (*f.*)	Loro to you	si yourselves	(per) Loro

The polite form of address in Italian is **Lɛi** (frequently written with a capital for greater politeness), with the third person singular form of the verb. The plural of **Lɛi** is **Loro.** Occasionally, in very formal address or correspondence, **Ella** (with the third person singular form of the verb) is used instead of **Lɛi.** The familiar form of address is **tu** in the singular (with the second person singular form of the verb), and **voi** in the plural (with the form of the verb in the second person plural). **Voi** is also used with a singular meaning (but with the verb in the plural) in business correspondence, and, in certain parts of Italy, in addressing equals and also servants, etc.

a) The Pronoun **ne**. **Ne**, which is not always translated into English, means *of it*, *of him*, *of her*, *of them*, *some* and *any* (*of them*), and it refers to somebody or something which has already been mentioned.

Ha sigarette? — **Sì, ne**	Do you have any cigarettes? —
hɔ due.	Yes, I have got two (of them).
Parla mai di suo fíglio?	Does she ever speak of her son?
— **Sì, ne parla spesso.**	— Yes, she often speaks of him.

b) Subject pronouns are used only for emphasis or contrast, or to avoid ambiguity. The subject neuter pronoun *it* is generally not expressed.

34. Object pronouns, except **loro**, are placed before the finite verb, or are attached to an infinitive (which loses its final **e**) or to a gerund. **Loro** always follows the verb and is never attached to it.

Lo vedo.	I see him.
Vɔglio vederlo.	I want to see it.
Stɔ guardandolo.	I am looking at it.
Parlo loro ogni giorno.	I speak to them every day.

35. Object pronouns follow affirmative imperatives, but preferably precede the negative commands. When an imperative ends in a stressed vowel, the initial consonant of the pronoun attached to it (**gli** excepted) is doubled.

Datemi questo.	Give me this one.
Non mi date quello.	Do not give me that one.
Fermiamoci!	Let us stop!
Dammi la mano.	Give me your hand.
Dagli il libro.	Give him the book.

EXCEPTIONS:

In commands with the **Lɛi**, **Loro** forms of address, the pronouns precede the verb (which in such cases is a form of the subjunctive).

> **Mi dia quello, non mi dia**   Give me that one, do not give
> **questo.**   me this one.
> **Non gli scrivano.**   Do not write him.

36. When there are two object pronouns

    a) The indirect precedes the direct.

    b) **mi, ti, si, ci, vi** become **me, te, se, ce, ve** respectively.

    c) **gli** and **le** become **glie** which combines with the direct
    object pronouns **lo, la, li, le,** and with **ne**:

    > **Me lo dice.**   He says it to me.
    > **Ce ne parla.**   He speaks of it to us.
    > **Glieli mando.**   I send them to him (her).
    > **Mandateglielo!**   Send it to him (her)!

    d) **loro**, as usual, follows the verb, and is written as a
    separate word:

    > **Ne parliamo loro.**   We speak of it to them

37. For the sake of emphasis and clearness, it is common to
    duplicate a subject, an object, etc., by means of a pronoun
    or an adverb:

    > **Gli avete parlato a Giovanni?**   Have you spoken to John?
    > **L'avete veduta mia madre?**   Have you seen my mother?
    > **Ci siete mai stato a Torino?**   Have you ever been in Turin?

38. **Ci, vi,** and **ne** are also used as unstressed adverbs of place.
    Ci and **vi** are interchangeable and mean *here* or *there*. **Ne**
    means *from there, thence.*

    > **Ɛ un buɔn ristorante; ci vado**   It is a good restaurant; I go
    > **spesso.**   there often.
    > **Sɛi stato da Carlo? — Sì, ne**   Have you been to Charles'
    > **vɛngo ora.**   house? — Yes, I am coming from there now.

39. Disjunctive Object Pronouns

They are used not only as objects of a preposition, but also for stress, and to avoid ambiguity:

Parla sεmpre di lεi.	He always speaks of her.
Ha chiamato lui, non lεi.	He called him, not her.
Questo ὲ il libro di lui.	This is his book.

Repetition is also used for stress:

Mi piace questo libro.	I like this book.
A me mi piace questo libro.	I like this book.

Lui, lεi, loro are frequently used instead of **egli, ella, essi, esse.**

40. Relative Pronouns

che who, whom, which, that (*subject and direct object*)
cui whom, which, that (*object of a preposition*)
cui (*preceded by the definite article*) whose
il (la) quale, i (le) quali who, whom, which, that (*frequently add clarity*)
chi (*or* **colui che**) he who, him who, one who, etc.
quεl che, quello che, ciɔ che what, that which

41. Interrogative Pronouns and Adjectives

che?	what? which? (*adjective*)
che?	
che cɔsa?	what? (*pronoun*)
cɔsa?	
che!	what a!
quale? quali?	which? (*adjective and pronoun*)
chi?	who? whom?
di chi?	whose?
quanto, -a?	how much?
quanti, -e?	how many?

42. Certain indefinite pronouns take the preposition **di** before an adjective or a noun:

Nulla di nuɔvo.	Nothing new.
Qualcɔsa di ưtile.	Something useful.

43. The Perfect Tenses

a) They are formed, as in English, by adding the past participle of the verb to various forms of the auxiliary **avere**, *to have*:

Hɔ parlato.	I have spoken, I spoke.
Avremo parlato.	We shall have spoken.
Avevano parlato.	They had spoken.

The past participle of verbs conjugated with **avere** agrees with a preceding direct object:

Li abbiamo veduti stamani.   We saw them this morning.

b) Several verbs however, especially those expressing motion, change, atmospheric conditions, etc., are conjugated with the auxiliary **ɛssere**, *to be*, and then the past participle agrees with the subject:

Rɔsa ɛ̀ arrivata.	Rose has arrived.
Eravamo stati al cinema.	We had been at the movies.
Stamani ɛ̀ piovuto.	This morning it rained.

44. The Pluperfect (Past Perfect). In Italian there are two pluperfects:

a) The one formed with the imperfect of the auxiliary:

Avevo finito di mangiare.   I had finished eating.

b) The one formed with the preterite (past absolute) of the auxiliary. The latter is used only after such conjunctions of time as **appena che**, *as soon as*, **quando**, *when*, **dopo che**, *after*, etc., when the main verb is in the preterite.

Quand'ɛbbi finito il pranzo   When I had finished dinner, I
andai al cinema.   went to the movies.

45. Tenses of the Verb (that differ from English)

a) The present indicative is often used for a future

(1) To indicate a definite or immediate act:

Domani parto.   I (shall) leave tomorrow.

(2) To ask for orders:

Che faccio?   What shall I do?

b) The imperfect indicative is used (1) in description; (2) to express a customary action or a condition in the past; and (3) to express action in progress when something else happened:

Il cielo era azzurro.	The sky was blue.
Andava a scuola tutte le mattine.	He used to go to school every morning.
Non lo sapevo.	I did not know (it).
Egli scriveva una lettera quando entrai.	He was writing a letter when I entered.

c) The present perfect and the preterite (past absolute) of the indicative both express a single (accomplished) act in the past, but with this difference:

(1) The preterite refers to an action that took place in the (distant) past, and has no relation to the present:

La guerra finì nel 1918.   The war ended in 1918.

(2) The present perfect (frequently introduced by ɔggi, *today*, **questa settimana**, *this week*, **questa mattina**, *this morning*, **questo mese**, *this month*, etc.) refers to an action which has taken place in the recent past, and is related to the present time:

Ɔggi hɔ scritto cinque lettere.   I have written five letters today.

d) The future (indicative) may be used idiomatically to express conjecture or probability in the present; the future perfect to express conjecture or probability in the past:

Che ora sarà?   What time can it be?
Sarà stata in casa.   She was probably in the house.

e) The conditional may be used similarly to express an unconfirmed report:

Secondo Enzo sua sorella   According to Enzo his sister is
sarebbe ammalata.   ill.
A quanto pare, il ponte   Apparently the bridge col-
sarebbe crollato.   lapsed.

f) The future is used after **se** and **quando** if it is implied in the English sentence:

Se mi inviteranno, non ac-   If they invite me, I shall not
cetterò   accept.
Quando andrò a Roma,   When I go to Rome, I shall
visiterò il Vaticano.   visit the Vatican.

46. The subjunctive is used in polite commands with the **Lei**, **Loro** forms of address (*see* § 71).

47. The subjunctive is used in wishes and exhortations:

Dio voglia!   May God grant it!
Magari lo sapessi!   Would that I knew it!
Che vengano!   Let them come!

48. In noun clauses the subjunctive is used

a) When the main-clause verb expresses volition, emotion, doubt, believing, etc.:

Voglio che lo faccia.   I want him to do it.
Temo che non arrivi.   I am afraid he will not (may not) arrive.
Dubita che lo sappia.   She doubts that he knows it.
Credo che abbiano torto.   I believe they are wrong.

b) After verbs of knowing when negative:

Non so se sia a casa.   I do not know whether she is home.

49. The subjunctive is used after impersonal expressions, except those denoting certainty:

> **È necessario che lo dica.** It is necessary that he say it.
> **Si dice che sia a Firenze.** They say he is in Florence.

The infinitive is sometimes used:

> **Mi è impossibile uscire.** It is impossible for me to go out.

50. The subjunctive is used in adverbial clauses expressing

a) Purpose:

> **Ve lo dirò perchè lo sappiate.** I will tell you so that you may know it.

b) Time:

> **Glielo dissi prima che partisse.** I told him before he left.
> **Aspetterò finchè ritorni.** I shall wait until she returns

With **finchè**, *until*, futurity must be implied.

c) Concession:

> **Benchè piova, usciremo lo stesso.** Although it is raining, we shall go out just the same.
> **Se mai venisse, fatelo entrare.** Should he come, let him in.

d) Condition:

> **Può uscire purchè ritorni prima delle dieci** She may go out provided she returns before ten o'clock.

e) In the "if" clauses of conditional sentences contrary to fact:

> **Se avessi il denaro, comprerei la casa.** If I had the money, I would buy the house.

51. The subjunctive is used in adjectival relative clauses

a) After an indefinite or negative antecedent:

> **Cerco un ragazzo che sappia l'italiano.** I am looking for a boy who knows Italian.

Non conosco nessuno che sia   I do not know anyone who
   stato là.   has been there.

b) After a relative superlative:

   È la più bɛlla città che *a*bbia   It is the most beautiful city
   mai visto.   I have ever seen.

52. The subjunctive is used after such indefinite words as:
chi*u*nque, *whoever*, **dov*u*nque**, *wherever*, **checchè**, *whatever*,
etc.:

   Chi*u*nque su*ɔ*ni il campanɛllo,   Whoever rings the bell, do
      non apra.   not open (the door),

53. When the main verb and the subordinate verb have the
same subject, the infinitive is generally used instead of a
subjunctive clause:

   Sono dolɛnte di ɛssere arri-   I am sorry I have arrived
      vato tardi.   late.

A few verbs allow the use of the infinitive (usually preceded by **di**) even when there is a change of subject:

dire	to say
permɛttere	to allow
pregare	to beg
proibire	to forbid
lasciare	to let
comandare	to command
	etc.

Mi disse di studiare.   He told me to study.

54. Sequence of Tenses

When the action of the subordinate verb takes place at
the same time or after that of the main verb, the subjunctive tenses to be used are as follows:

$$\text{Le} \begin{cases} \textbf{dico} \\ \textbf{dir\textipa{ɔ}} \\ \textbf{h\textipa{ɔ} detto} \end{cases} \quad \textbf{che se ne vada} \ (\textit{pres. subj.})$$

$$\text{Le} \begin{cases} \textbf{dicevo} \\ \textbf{dissi} \\ \textbf{dir}\epsilon\textbf{i} \\ \textbf{avevo detto} \end{cases} \textbf{che se ne andasse} \ (\textit{imp. subj.})$$

When the action of the subordinate verb is prior to that of the main verb, the present subjunctive in the above cases is replaced by the perfect subjunctive or the imperfect subjunctive, and the imperfect subjunctive is replaced by the pluperfect subjunctive:

$$\text{T}\epsilon\textbf{mo che l'} \begin{cases} \textit{a}\textbf{bbia udito.} \\ \textbf{udisse.} \end{cases} \quad \text{I am afraid he (has) heard it.}$$

Temevo che l'avesse udito.   I was afraid he had heard it.

55. The infinitive is used instead of the English present participle

a) After a preposition:

Uscì senza parlarmi.   He went away without speaking to me.

Al + the infinitive is *on* + the gerund:

All'uscire di casa, chiuse la porta.   On leaving the house, he closed the door.

b) As the subject of a verb:

Il mangiare molto fa male.   Eating (too) much is bad.

c) After **vedere, udire, sentire**, etc.:

Lo vedo venire.   I see him coming.

56. The present participle is used to express manner (with no preposition):

Impariamo studiando.   We learn by studying.

57. **Stare** is used with the gerund to form progressive tenses:

Stavamo mangiando quando Lɛi entrɔ.   We were eating when you entered.

58. The true passive voice is formed with the verb **essere** (occasionally **andare** and **venire**) and the past participle:

> **Il fucile fu pulito dal soldato.**   The gun was cleaned by the soldier.

59. The true passive is replaced by a reflexive construction which may assume the following forms:

a) The verb agrees in number with the subject:

> **Qui si parla italiano.**   Italian is spoken here (*lit.* "Italian speaks itself here").
> **Si bruciarono due case.**   Two houses were burned.

In this construction the verb generally precedes the subject.

b) When the subject is impersonal ("one," "people"), the verb is always singular:

> **Si mangia bene qui.**   The food is good here (*lit.* "One eats well here").
> **Si paga alla cassa.**   One pays at the (cashier's) desk.

c) Note that in such cases, although **essere** is used in the singular, it is followed by a plural adjective:

> **Si è attivi in questa città.**   One is active in this city.

The same construction is possible with such verbs as **rimanere**, *to remain*, **diventare**, *to become*, etc.

60. The reflexive pronouns are used

a) As in English:

> **M'inganno.**   I deceive myself.

b) With no reflexive meaning:

> **Se ne andò.**   He went away.
> **Ci addormentammo.**   We fell asleep.
> **Si pentono.**   They repent.

c) Instead of the English possessive with parts of the body or one's clothing:

Si lava le mani.	He washes his hands.
Si mette il cappello.	She is putting on her hat.

61. The verb **piacere**, *to like*, takes the indirect object:

Il latte non mi (gli, le, ci, *etc.***) piace.**	I (he, she, we) do not like milk (*lit.* "Milk is not pleasing to me [to him, to her, to us, etc.]").
Mi (gli, le, ci, *etc.***) piacciono le rose.**	I (he, she, we, etc.) like roses (*lit.* "Roses are pleasing to me [to him, to her, to us, etc.]").

Note that what is the subject in English becomes the indirect object in Italian

62. Uses of the preposition **da**

Besides translating the English prepositions *from* and *by*, **da** may be used as follows:

a) In expressions of time (note tenses in both Italian and English):

Sono qui da due anni (Also: **Sono due anni che sono qui**).	I *have been* here two years.
Ero qui da due anni (Also: **Erano due anni che ero qui**).	I *had been* here two years.

b) Before an infinitive, to express purpose, obligation, necessity, etc.:

Ho molto da fare.	I have a lot to do.
Non hanno niente da mangiare	They have nothing to eat.

c) Before a noun to express purpose, fitness, manner, etc.:

Un biglietto da visita.	A calling card.

Un vestito da sera.	An evening dress.
Vivere da signore.	To live like a rich man.

d) Before a noun preceded by the definite article, to express a personal characteristic:

La ragazza dai capelli biondi.	The girl with blond hair.

e) To denote *at* (or *to*) *the house* (*office, shop,* etc.) *of*:

Vado da Maria.	I am going to Mary's house.
Era dal parrucchiere.	He was at the barber's.

f) With the meaning of *as, like, in the manner of*:

Io farò da guida.	I shall act as a guide.

63. The prepositions **in** and **a**

a) Before names of countries, continents, large islands, etc., the preposition **in** translates both the English *in* and *to*.

Siamo in America.	We are in America.
Vanno in Italia.	They are going to Italy.

For use and omission of definite article in this connection see § 2*c*.

b) Before names of cities, the preposition **a** translates both the English *in* and *to*:

È a Roma.	He is in Rome.
Andiamo a Napoli.	We are going to Naples.

64. The following three verbs are also used as modal auxiliaries, that is, they can be followed by an infinitive without a preposition:

potere	to be able to, can, may
dovere	to have to, must
volere	to want

Possiamo partire.	We may leave.
Dovremmo lavorare.	We should work.
Volevano comprare una casa.	They wanted to buy a house.

In the compound tenses **potere, dovere,** and **volere** take the
auxiliary of the complementary infinitive:

Non hɔ potuto capirlo.   I was unable to understand him.
Non è voluto ritornare.   He did not want to return.

65. Idiomatic uses of **dovere**

a) **dovere** + the infinitive = *to be to* or *to be going to* or
shall (*will*) + the infinitive:

Dɛve farlo domani.   He is to (is going to, will) do it tomorrow.

b) **dɛvo (dobbiamo)** + the infinitive in a question = *shall I*
(*shall we*) + the infinitive:

Dɛvo ritornare domani?   Shall I return tomorrow?

66. Idiomatic uses of **avere,** *to have*

a) **Avere** + the noun = *to be* + the adjective:

	fame	hungry
	sete	thirsty
	sonno	sleepy
	paura	afraid
hɔ	ragione I am	right
	tɔrto	wrong
	fretta	in a hurry
	caldo	warm
	freddo	cold

b) With parts of the body:

Hɔ gli ɔcchi neri.   My eyes are black.
Hɔ le mani pulite.   My hands are clean.

c) To express age:

Hɔ venti anni.   I am twenty years old.

67. Idiomatic uses of **fare,** *to do* or *to make*

a) **fare** + the infinitive + noun = *to have* + noun + past participle:

Faccio pulire la casa.   I am having the house cleaned.
Si fece tagliare i capelli.   He had his hair cut.

b) In expressions of weather:

fa	bɛl tempo		it is	good weather
	cattivo tɛmpo			bad weather
	caldo			warm
	freddo			cold
	fresco			cool

EXCEPTIONS:

c'ɛ il sole	it is sunny	ɛ sereno	it is clear (fair)
c'ɛ la nebbia	it is foggy		weather
c'ɛ fango	it is muddy	ɛ nuvolo	it is cloudy
c'ɛ polvere	it is dusty	ɛ copɛrto	it is overcast
tira vɛnto	it is windy		

c) In expressions of time

(1) The time element + **fa** = time element + *ago*:

Morì due anni fa.   He died two years ago.

(2) When **fare** precedes the time element, it must agree:

Domani farà un mese che partì.   It will be one month tomorrow since he went away.

Domani faranno due mesi che partì.   It will be two months tomorrow since he went away.

68. Regular Verbs: three conjugations

INFINITIVE

I		II
parlare (to) speak		**vendere** (to) sell
	III	
	finire (to) finish	

PRESENT PARTICIPLE

I		II
parlando speaking		**vendɛndo** selling
	III	
	finɛndo finishing	

PAST PARTICIPLE

I		II
parlato spoken		**venduto** sold
	III	
	finito finished	

69. The Simple Tenses

INDICATIVE MODE

PRESENT

io **parl o**   I speak, am speaking, do speak
tu **parl i**   you (*familiar*) speak, etc.
lei, lui, Lei **parl a**   you (*polite*), he, she, it speak(s), etc.
noi **parl iamo**   we speak, etc.
voi **parl ate**   you (*familiar and semipolite*) speak, etc.
loro, Loro **parl ano**   they, you (*polite*) speak, etc.

vend o	I sell, am selling, do sell, etc.	**fin isc o**[2]	I finish, am finishing, do finish, etc
vend i		**fin isc i**	
vend e		**fin isc e**	
vend iamo		**fin iamo**	
vend ete		**fin ite**	
vend ono		**fin isc ono**	

IMPERFECT (Past Descriptive)
(Except for vowel characteristic of infinitive,
endings are identical for the three conjugations.)

parl avo   I was speaking, used to speak, spoke, etc.
parl avi
parl ava
parl avamo
parl avate
parl avano

vend evo	I was selling, used to sell, sold, etc.	**fin ivo**	I was finishing, used to finish, finished, etc.
vend evi		**fin ivi**	
vend eva		**fin iva**	
vend evamo		**fin ivamo**	
vend evate		**fin ivate**	
vend evano		**fin ivano**	

[2] Many verbs of the 3rd conjugation do not add **isc** in the present indicative, imperative, and present subjunctive.

PRETERITE (Past Absolute)

I spoke, did speak, etc.	I sold, did sell, etc.	I finished, did finish, etc.
parl ai	vend ei	fin ii
parl asti	vend esti	fin isti
parl ɔ	vend è	fin ì
parl ammo	vend emmo	fin immo
parl aste	vend este	fin iste
parl *a*rono	vend *e*rono	fin *i*rono

FUTURE

(endings of three conjugations identical, added
to infinitive after dropping final e[3])

I shall (will) speak, etc.	I shall (will) sell, etc.	I shall (will) finish, etc.
parler ɔ	vender ɔ	finir ɔ
parler ai	vender ai	finir ai
parler à	vender à	finir à
parler emo	vender emo	finir emo
parler ete	vender ete	finir ete
parler anno	vender anno	finir anno

CONDITIONAL

(endings of three conjugations identical, added
to infinitive after dropping final e[3])

I should (would) speak, etc.	I should (would) sell, etc.	I should (would) finish, etc.
parler ɛi	vender ɛi	finir ɛi
parler esti	vender esti	finir esti
parler ɛbbe	vender ɛbbe	finir ɛbbe
parler emmo	vender emmo	finir emmo
parler este	vender este	finir este
parler ɛbbero	vender ɛbbero	finir ɛbbero

SUBJUNCTIVE MODE

PRESENT

(che) parl i	vend a	fin isc a

---

[3] Note, however, that with the exception of **dare, fare, stare,** the verbs of the
first conjugation change the **a** of the infinitive to **e**.

parl i	vend a	fin isc a
parl i	vend a	fin isc a
parl iamo	vend iamo	fin iamo
parl iate	vend iate	fin iate
parl ino	vend ano	fin *isc* ano

IMPERFECT (Past)
(Except for vowel characteristic of infinitive, endings
are identical for the three conjugations.)

(che) parl assi	vend essi	fin issi
parl assi	vend essi	fin issi
parl asse	vend esse	fin isse
parl *a*ssimo	vend *e*ssimo	fin *i*ssimo
parl aste	vend este	fin iste
parl *a*ssero	vend *e*ssero	fin *i*ssero

70. The Compound Tenses (Perfect tenses)

PERFECT INFINITIVE

avere $\begin{cases} \textbf{parlato} \\ \textbf{venduto} \\ \textbf{finito} \end{cases}$ to have $\begin{cases} \text{spoken} \\ \text{sold} \\ \text{finished} \end{cases}$

εssere[4] arrivato   to have arrived

PERFECT PARTICIPLE

avεndo $\begin{cases} \textbf{parlato} \\ \textbf{venduto} \\ \textbf{finito} \end{cases}$ having $\begin{cases} \text{spoken} \\ \text{sold} \\ \text{finished} \end{cases}$

essεndo arrivato   having arrived

INDICATIVE MODE

PRESENT PERFECT
(Present of **avere** [or **εssere**] + past participle)

---

[4] Intransitive verbs (especially those of motion) are conjugated with **εssere**.
Here **arrivare** is listed as a model.

hɔ		I have spoken, been speaking, etc.,
hai		sold, finished
ha	parlato	
	venduto	
abbiamo	finito	
avete		
hanno		

sono	arrivato (-a) I have arrived, etc.
sɛi	arrivato (-a)
ɛ̀	arrivato (-a)
siamo	arrivati (-e)
siete	arrivato (-a, -i, -e)
sono	arrivati (-e)

PLUPERFECT
(Past Perfect = Imperfect of **avere** [or **ɛssere**] + past participle)

avevo	I had spoken, etc.,	ɛro	arrivato (-a)	I had
avevi	sold, finished	ɛri	arrivato (-a)	arrived,
aveva	parlato	ɛra	arrivato (-a)	etc.
	venduto			
avevamo	finito	eravamo arrivati (-e)		
avevate		eravate arrivato (-a, -i, -e)		
avevano		ɛrano arrivati (-e)		

SECOND PLUPERFECT
(Second Past Perfect = Preterite of **avere** [or **ɛssere**] + past participle)

ɛbbi	I had spoken, etc.,	fui	arrivato (-a)	I had
avesti	sold, finished	fosti	arrivato (-a)	arrived,
ɛbbe	parlato	fu	arrivato (-a)	etc.
	venduto			
avemmo	finito	fummo arrivati (-e)		
aveste		foste arrivato (-a, -i, -e)		
ɛbbero		furono arrivati (-e)		

FUTURE PERFECT

avrò	I shall have spoken, etc.	sarò	I shall have
avrai	sold, finished	sarai	arrived,
avrà	parlato	sarà	etc.
avremo	venduto	saremo	arrivato (-a),
avrete	finito	sarete	etc.
avranno		saranno	

CONDITIONAL PERFECT

avrɛi	I should (would)	sarɛi	I should (would)
avresti	have spoken, etc.,	saresti	have arrived
avrɛbbe	sold, finished	sarɛbbe	etc.
	parlato		arrivato (-a),
avremmo	venduto	saremmo	etc.
avreste	finito	sareste	
avrɛbbero		sarɛbbero	

SUBJUNCTIVE MODE

PRESENT PERFECT

abbia		sia	
abbia		sia	
abbia	parlato	sia	
	venduto		arrivato (-a), etc.
abbiamo	finito	siamo	
abbiate		siate	
abbiano		siano	

PLUPERFECT (Past Perfect)

avessi		fossi	
avessi		fossi	
avesse	parlato	fosse	
	venduto		arrivato (-a), etc.
avessimo	finito	fossimo	
aveste		foste	
avessero		fossero	

71. Imperative Mode

	I		II		III	
Familiar sing.	**parl a**	} speak	**vend i**	} sell	**fin isc i**	} finish
Familiar	**parl ate**		**vend ete**		**fin ite**	

pl. and
semipolite
sing. and pl.

	parl iamo	**vend iamo**	**fin iamo**
	let us speak	let us sell	let us finish
Polite sing.	**parl i**	**vend a**	**fin isc a**
	speak	sell	finish
Polite pl.	**parl ino**	**vend ano**	**fin isc ano**
	speak	sell	finish

Note that the command forms for **Lɛi** and **Loro** are real subjunctives.

a) The negative imperative of the familiar singular is an infinitive:

Parla! Speak!   **Non parlare!** Do not speak!

b) In elliptical sentences the infinitive preceded by **a** is sometimes used as an imperative:

A mangiare! Come and eat!   Let us go and eat!

c) For position of object pronouns with the imperative, see § 35.

72. Progressive Tenses

The various tenses of **stare** (sometimes **andare**) combine with the present participle to form the progressive tenses of other verbs:

stɔ (stavo, etc.) **parlando, ven-**   I am (was, etc.) speaking,
dɛndo, finɛndo, etc.   selling, finishing, etc.

73. Orthographic (Spelling) Changes in Verbs

a) Verbs whose infinitives

End with	Add	Before	Examples
1. **-care** ⎫	**h**	**e** or **i**	**cercare**
2. **-gare** ⎭			**pagare**

PRES. IND.	cerco, **cerchi**, cerca, **cerchiamo**, cercate, cercano
	pago, **paghi**, paga, **paghiamo**, pagate, pagano
FUTURE	cercherò, etc.; **pagherò**, etc.
CONDITIONAL	cercherɛi, etc.; **pagherɛi**, etc.
IMPERATIVE	cerca, **cerchiamo**, cercate, **cerchi** (Lɛi), **cerchino** (Loro)
	paga, **paghiamo**, pagate, **paghi** (Lɛi), **paghino** (Loro)
PRES. SUBJ.	**cerchi**, etc.; **paghi**, etc.

b) Verbs whose infinitives

End with	Drop	Before	Examples
1. **-ciare** ⎫	**i**	**e** or **i**	**cominciare**
2. **-giare** ⎭			**mangiare**
3. other verbs in **-iare**	**i**	**i**	**fischiare**

PRES. IND.	comincio, **cominci**, comincia, **cominciamo**, cominciate, cominciano
	mangio **mangi**, mangia, **mangiamo**, mangiate, mangiano
	fischio, **fischi**, fischia, **fischiamo**, fischiate, fischiano
FUTURE	comincerò, etc.; **mangerò**, etc.
CONDITIONAL	comincerɛi, etc.; **mangerɛi**, etc.
IMPERATIVE	comincia,ⁱ **cominciamo**, cominciate, **cominci** (Lɛi), **comincino** (Loro)
	mangia, **mangiamo**, mangiate, **mangi** (Lɛi), **mangino** (Loro)
	fischia, **fischiamo**, fischiate, **fischi** (Lɛi), **fischino** (Loro)
PRES. SUBJ.	**cominci**, etc.; **mangi**, etc.; **fischi**, etc.

c) Verbs whose infinitives end in **-cere** take an **i** before the **u** of the past participle:

giacere: giaciuto   **conoscere: conosciuto**

74. Conjugation of a Reflexive Verb

INFINITIVE	**lavarsi**, to wash oneself
PRES. IND.	mi lavo, ti lavi, si lava, ci laviamo, vi lavate, si *la*vano
PRETERITE	mi lavai ,etc.
IMP. IND.	mi lavavo, etc.
FUTURE	mi laverò, etc.
CONDITIONAL	mi laverɛi, etc.
IMPERATIVE	*la*vati, si lavi (Lɛi), lavi*a*moci, lav*a*tevi, si *la*vino (Loro)
PRES. PERFECT	mi sono lavato (-a), ti sɛi lavato (-a), s'ɛ̀ lavato (-a), ci siamo lavati (-e), vi siete lavato (-a, -i, -e), si sono lavati (-e)
PRES. SUBJ.	mi lavi, etc.
IMP. SUBJ.	mi lavassi, etc.
GERUND	lav*a*ndosi
PAST PARTICIPLE	lav*a*tosi

75. Some Common Irregular Verbs

Verbs preceded by * are conjugated with **ɛssere**. The forms not listed are regular. The command forms of **Lɛi** and **Loro** are not listed because they can be derived from the present subjunctive.

1. ***andare, andando, andato**, to go

PRES. IND.	vado *or* vɔ, vai, va, andiamo, andate, vanno
PRES. SUBJ.	vada, etc., andiamo, andiate, v*a*dano
FUT.	andrò, andrai, etc.
COND.	andrɛi, andresti, etc.
IMPERATIVE	va', andiamo, andate

2. **aprire, aprɛndo, apɛrto**, to open

3. **avere, avɛndo, avuto**, to have

PRES. IND.	hɔ, hai, ha, abbiamo, avete, hanno

PRES. SUBJ.	*a*bbia, etc., abbiamo, abbiate, *a*bbiano
FUT.	avr*ɔ*, avrai, etc.
COND.	avrɛi, avresti, etc.
PRET.	ɛbbi, avesti, ɛbbe, avemmo, aveste, ɛbbero
IMPERATIVE	abbi, abbiamo, abbiate

4. **bere, bevɛndo, bevuto,** to drink

PRES. IND.	bevo, bevi, beve, beviamo, bevete, bevono
PRES. SUBJ.	beva, etc., beviamo, beviate, bevano
FUT.	berr*ɔ*, berrai, etc.
COND.	berrɛi, berresti, etc.
IMP. IND.	bevevo, bevevi, etc.
PRET.	bevvi, bevesti, bevve, bevemmo, beveste, bevvero
IMP. SUBJ.	bevessi, etc.
IMPERATIVE	bevi, beviamo, bevete

5. ***cadere, cadɛndo, caduto,** to fall

FUT.	cadr*ɔ*, cadrai, etc.
COND.	cadrɛi, cadresti, etc.
PRET.	caddi, cadesti, cadde, cademmo, cadeste, caddero

6. **chiɛdere, chiedɛndo, chiɛsto,** to ask

PRET.	chiɛsi, chiedesti, chiɛse, chiedemmo, chiedeste, chiɛsero

7. **chi*u*dere, chiudɛndo, chiuso,** to close

PRET.	chiusi, chiudesti, chiuse, chiudemmo, chiudeste, chi*u*sero

8. **con*o*scere, conoscɛndo, conosciuto,** to know

PRET.	conobbi, conoscesti, conobbe, conoscemmo, conosceste, con*o*bbero

9. ***c*o*rrere, corrɛndo, corso,** to run (sometimes conjugated with **avere**)

PRET.	corsi, corresti, corse, corremmo, correste, c*o*rsero

10. **dare, dando, dato,** to give

PRES. IND.	d*ɔ*, dai, dà, diamo, date, danno
PRES. SUBJ.	dia, etc., diamo, diate, d*i*ano
FUT.	dar*ɔ*, darai, etc.
COND.	darɛi, daresti, etc.
PRET.	diɛdi *or* dɛtti, desti, diɛde *or* dɛtte, demmo, deste, diɛdero *or* dɛttero

IMP. SUBJ.   dessi, etc.
IMPERATIVE   da', diamo, date

11. **dire, dicɛndo, detto,** to tell, say
PRES. IND.   dico, dici, dice, diciamo, dite, dicono
PRES. SUBJ.   dica, etc., diciamo, diciate, dicano
IMP. IND.   dicevo, dicevi, etc.
PRET.   dissi, dicesti, disse, dicemmo, diceste
                dissero
IMP. SUBJ.   dicessi, etc.
IMPERATIVE   di', diamo, dite

12. ***dolere, dolɛndo, doluto,** to ache, pain
PRES. IND.   dɔlgo, duɔli, duɔle, doliamo, dolete, dɔl-
                gono
PRES. SUBJ.   dɔlga, etc., doliamo, doliate, dɔlgano
FUT.   dorrɔ̀, dorrai, etc.
COND.   dorrɛi, dorresti, etc.
PRET.   dɔlsi, dolesti, dɔlse, dolemmo, doleste,
                dɔlsero

13. **dovere, dovɛndo, dovuto,** to have to, must (*see* § 64)
PRES. IND.   dɛvo, dɛvi, dɛve, dobbiamo, dovete,
                dɛvono
PRES. SUBJ.   dɛva, etc., dobbiamo, dobbiate, dɛvano
FUT.   dovrɔ̀, dovrai, etc.
COND.   dovrei, dovresti, etc.

14. ***ɛssere, essɛndo, stato,** to be
PRES. IND.   sono, sɛi, è, siamo, siete, sono
PRES. SUBJ.   sia, etc., siamo, siate, siano
FUT.   sarɔ̀, sarai, etc.
COND.   sarɛi, saresti, etc.
IMP. IND.   ɛro, ɛri, ɛra, eravamo, eravate, ɛrano
PRET.   fui, fosti, fu, fummo, foste, furono
IMP. SUBJ.   fossi, etc.
IMPERATIVE   sii, siamo, siate

15. **fare, facɛndo, fatto,** to do, make
PRES. IND.   faccio or fɔ, fai, fa, facciamo, fate, fanno
PRES. SUBJ.   faccia, etc., facciamo, facciate, facciano
FUT.   farɔ̀, farai, etc.
COND.   farɛi, faresti, etc.
IMP. IND.   facevo, facevi, etc.

PRET. feci, facesti, fece, facemmo, faceste, fecero
IMP. SUBJ. facessi, etc.
IMPERATIVE fa', facciamo, fate

16. *giungere, giungɛndo, giunto, to arrive
PRET. giunsi, giungesti, giunse, giungemmo, giungeste, giunsero

17. lɛggere, leggɛndo, lɛtto, to read
PRET. lɛssi, leggesti, lɛsse, leggemmo, leggeste, lɛssero

18. mɛttere, mettɛndo, messo, to put
PRET. misi, mettesti, mise, mettemmo, metteste misero

19. *nascere, nascɛndo, nato, to be born
PRET. nacqui, nascesti, nacque, nascemmo, nasceste, nacquero

20. *piacere, piacɛndo, piaciuto, to please (like)
PRES. IND. piaccio, piaci, piace, piacciamo, piacete, piacciono
PRES. SUBJ. piaccia, etc., piacciamo, piacciate, piacciano
PRET. piacqui, piacesti, piacque, piacemmo, piaceste, piacquero

21. potere, potɛndo, potuto, to be able, can, may (see § 64)
PRES. IND. pɔsso, puɔi, puɔ, possiamo, potete, pɔssono
PRES. SUBJ. pɔssa, etc., possiamo, possiate, pɔssano
FUT. potrɔ, potrai, etc.
COND. potrɛi, potresti, etc.

22. prɛndere, prendɛndo, prɛso, to take
PRET. presi, prendesti, prese, prendemmo, prendeste, presero

23. rídere, ridɛndo, riso, to laugh
PRET. risi, ridesti, rise, ridemmo, rideste, rísero

24. *rimanere, rimanɛndo, rimasto, to remain
PRES. IND. rimango, rimani, rimane, rimaniamo, rimanete, rimangono
PRES. SUBJ. rimanga, etc., rimaniamo, rimaniate, rimangano
FUT. rimarrɔ, rimarrai, etc.
COND. rimarrɛi, rimarresti, etc.

PRET.   rimasi, rimanesti, rimase, rimanemmo rimaneste, rimasero

25. **rispondere, rispondɛndo, risposto,** to answer
PRET.   risposi, rispondesti, rispose, rispondemmo, rispondeste, risposero

26. **rompere, rompɛndo, rotto,** to break
PRET.   ruppi, rompesti, ruppe, rompemmo, rompeste, ruppero

27. ***salire, salɛndo, salito,** to go up (when used transitively it is conjugated with **avere**, when used intransitively with **ɛssere**)
PRES. IND.   salgo, sali, sale, saliamo, salite, salgono
PRES. SUBJ.   salga, etc., saliamo, saliate, salgano

28. **sapere, sapɛndo, saputo,** to know
PRES. IND.   sɔ, sai, sa, sappiamo, sapete, sanno
PRES. SUBJ.   sappia, etc., sappiamo, sappiate, sappiano
FUT.   saprɔ, saprai, etc.
COND.   saprɛi, sapresti, etc.
PRET.   sɛppi, sapesti, sɛppe, sapemmo, sapeste, sɛppero
IMPERATIVE   sappi, sappiamo, sappiate

29. ***scendere, scendɛndo, sceso,** to descend (when used transitively it is conjugated with **avere**, when used intransitively, with **ɛssere**)
PRET.   scesi, scendesti, scese, scendemmo, scendeste, scesero

30. **scrivere, scrivɛndo, scritto,** to write
PRET.   scrissi, scrivesti, scrisse, scrivemmo, scriveste, scrissero

31. **sedere, sedɛndo, seduto,** to sit
PRES. IND.   siɛdo *or* sɛggo, siɛdi, siɛde, sediamo, sedete siɛdono *or* sɛggono
PRES. SUBJ.   siɛda *or* sɛgga, etc., sediamo, sediate, siɛdano *or* sɛggano
IMPERATIVE   siɛdi, sediamo, sedete

32. **spɛndere, spendɛndo, speso,** to spend
PRET.   spesi, spendesti, spese, spendemmo, spendeste, spesero

33. *stare, stando, stato, to stay, be
PRES. IND.   stɔ, stai, sta, stiamo, state, stanno
PRES. SUBJ.   stia, etc., stiamo, stiate, stiano
FUT.   starɔ̀, starai, etc.
COND.   starɛi, staresti, etc.
PRET.   stɛtti, stesti, stɛtte, stemmo, steste, stɛttero
IMP. SUBJ.   stessi, etc.
IMPERATIVE   sta', stiamo, state

34. tenere, tenɛndo, tenuto, to keep, hold
PRES. IND.   tɛngo, tiɛni, tiɛne, teniamo, tenete, tɛngono
PRES. SUBJ.   tɛnga, etc., teniamo, teniate, tɛngano
FUT.   terrɔ̀, terrai, etc.
COND.   terrɛi, terresti, etc.
PRET.   tenni, tenesti, tenne, tenemmo, teneste, tennero
IMPERATIVE   tiɛni, teniamo, tenete

35. tɔgliere, togliɛndo, tɔlto, to take from, take away
PRES. IND.   tɔlgo, tɔgli, tɔglie, togliamo, togliete, tɔlgono
PRES. SUBJ.   tɔlga, etc., togliamo, togliate, tɔlgano
FUT.   torrɔ̀, torrai, etc.
COND.   torrɛi, torresti, etc.
PRET.   tɔlsi, togliesti, tɔlse, togliemmo, toglieste, tɔlsero
IMPERATIVE   tɔgli, togliamo, togliete

36. *uscire, uscɛndo, uscito, to go out
PRES. IND.   ɛsco, ɛsci, ɛsce, usciámo, uscite, ɛscono
PRES. SUBJ.   ɛsca, etc., usciamo, usciate, ɛscano
IMPERATIVE   ɛsci, usciamo, uscite

37. vedere, vedɛndo, visto or veduto, to see
FUT.   vedrɔ̀, vedrai, etc.
COND.   vedrɛi, vedresti, etc.
PRET.   vidi, vedesti, vide, vedemmo, vedeste, vídero

38. *venire, venɛndo, venuto, to come
PRES. IND.   vɛngo, viɛni, viɛne, veniamo, venite, vɛngono
PRES. SUBJ.   vɛnga, etc., veniamo, veniate, vɛngano

FUT.	verrò, verrai, etc.
COND.	verrɛi, verresti, etc.
PRET.	venni, venisti, venne, venimmo, veniste, vennero
IMPERATIVE	viɛni, veniamo, venite

39. *vivere, vivɛndo, vissuto, to live (sometimes conjugated with avere)

FUT.	vivrò, vivrai, etc.
COND.	vivrɛi, vivresti, etc.
PRET.	vissi, vivesti, visse, vivemmo, viveste, vissero

40. volere, volɛndo, voluto, to want (see § 64)

PRES. IND.	vɔglio, vuɔi, vuɔle, vogliamo, volete vɔgliono
PRES. SUBJ.	vɔglia, etc., vogliamo, vogliate, vɔgliano
FUT.	vorrò, vorrai, etc.
COND.	vorrɛi, vorresti, etc.
PRET.	vɔlli, volesti, vɔlle, volemmo, voleste vɔllero
IMPERATIVE.	vɔgli, vogliamo, vogliate

76. Cardinal Numerals

1	uno	28	ventɔtto
2	due	29	ventinɔve
3	tre	30	trenta
4	quattro	31	trentuno
5	cinque	32	trentadue
6	sɛi	40	quaranta
7	sɛtte	50	cinquanta
8	ɔtto	60	sessanta
9	nɔve	70	settanta
10	diɛci	80	ottanta
11	undici	90	novanta
12	dodici	100	cɛnto
13	tredici	101	cɛnto uno
14	quattordici	102	cɛnto due
15	quindici	200	duecɛnto
16	sedici	300	trecɛnto

17 diciassette	400 quattrocento
18 diciotto	500 cinquecento
19 diciannove	600 seicento
20 venti	700 settecento
21 ventuno	800 ottocento
22 ventidue	900 novecento
23 ventitrè	1000 mille
24 ventiquattro	1500 mille cinquecento
25 venticinque	2000 due mila
26 ventisei	3000 tre mila
27 ventisette	1,000,000 un milione

77. Ordinal Numerals

1st	primo
2nd	secondo
3rd	terzo
4th	quarto
5th	quinto
6th	sesto
7th	settimo
8th	ottavo
9th	nono
10th	decimo
11th	undicesimo *or* decimo primo
12th	dodicesimo *or* decimo secondo
13th	tredicesimo *or* decimo terzo
14th	quattordicesimo *or* decimo quarto
15th	quindicesimo *or* decimo quinto
16th	sedicesimo *or* decimo sesto
17th	diciassettesimo *or* decimo settimo
18th	diciottesimo *or* decimo ottavo
19th	diciannovesimo *or* decimo nono
20th	ventesimo
21st	ventunesimo *or* ventesimo primo
22nd	ventiduesimo *or* ventesimo secondo
23rd	ventitreesimo *or* ventesimo terzo
24th	ventiquattresimo *or* ventesimo quarto
30th	trentesimo
70th	settantesimo
100th	centesimo

1000th millesimo
2000th duemillesimo
1,000,000th milionesimo

Note that after 10th, one can easily get any ordinal numeral, merely by dropping the last vowel of a given cardinal numeral, and adding -esimo. If a cardinal numeral ends in -tre (*three*), the final e is retained. Ordinal numerals are adjectives and agree with the noun in gender and number.

78.

1 centimeter (cent*i*metro) = .393 inches
1 inch (pollice *m.*) = 2.54 centimeters
1 meter (metro) = 39.37 inches or 3.28 feet or 1.093 yards
1 foot (piede *m.*) = .304 meters
1 yard = .914 meters
1 kilometer (chilometro) (km.) = .621 miles
1 mile (m*i*glio *m.*; *pl.* le m*i*glia) = 1.609 kilometers

1 liter (litro) = 2.113 pints or 1.056 quarts or .264 gallons
1 pint = .473 liters
1 quart = .946 liters
1 gallon = 3.785 liters

1 gram (grammo) = .035 ounces
1 ounce (*o*ncia) = 28.35 grams
1 kilogram (chilogrammo or chilo) = 2.204 pounds or 35.273 ounces
1 pound (libbra) = .453 kilograms

32 degrees (gradi) Fahrenheit (F) = 0° centigrade (centigrado)
100° C = 180° F
1° C = 1.8° F

To change degrees F to degrees C, subtract 32 and multiply by $\frac{5}{9}$ $(F - 32) \times \frac{5}{9} = C$

To change degrees C to degrees F, multiply by $\frac{9}{5}$ and add 32. $(C \times \frac{9}{5}) + 32 = F$

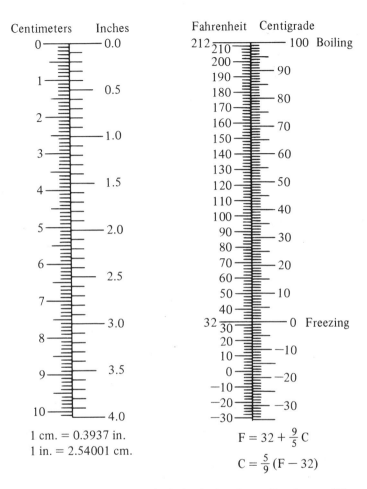

Centimeters   Inches

0	0.0
1	0.5
2	1.0
3	1.5
4	
5	2.0
6	2.5
7	3.0
8	
9	3.5
10	4.0

1 cm. = 0.3937 in.
1 in. = 2.54001 cm.

Fahrenheit   Centigrade

212 — 100 Boiling
32 — 0 Freezing

$$F = 32 + \frac{9}{5} C$$

$$C = \frac{5}{9} (F - 32)$$

79. A few place names and their derivative adjectives. (The English equivalent is omitted when meaning is apparent.)

l'Argentina	argentino
il Belgio	belga
Bologna	bolognese
il Brasile	brasiliano
il Canadà	canadese
la Cina	cinese

l'Egitto	egiziano
l'Europa	europeo
Firenze (*Florence*)	fiorentino
la Francia	francese
Genova (*Genoa*)	genovese
la Germania	tedesco (*German*)
il Giappone (*Japan*)	giapponese
la Grecia	greco
l'Inghilterra (*England*)	inglese
l'Irlanda	irlandese (*Irish*)
l'Italia	italiano
il Messico	messicano
Milano	milanese
Napoli (*Naples*)	napoletano
la Norvegia (*Norway*)	norvegese
l'Olanda (*Holland*)	olandese
Palermo	palermitano
la Polonia (*Poland*)	polacco
il Portogallo	portoghese
Roma	romano
la Russia	russo
la Sicilia	siciliano
la Svezia (*Sweden*)	svedese
la Svizzera (*Switzerland*)	svizzero
la Toscana (*Tuscany*)	toscano
la Turchia (*Turkey*)	turco
l'Ungheria (*Hungary*)	ungherese
Venezia (*Venice*)	veneziano

80. Lettere   Letters

INTESTAZIONE	HEADING
Egregio (Gentilissimo) Signore,	Dear Sir: } business
Egregio (Pregiatissimo) Signor A,	Dear Mr. A: } letters
Gentilissimo (Stimatissimo) Signor B,	My dear Mr. B,
(Mio) caro amico,	(My) dear friend,
Carissimo amico,	(My) dear friend,
Carissima Luisa,	(My) dear Louise,

CHIUSA	ENDING
Con distinti saluti, Distinti saluti,	} Yours truly, etc.
Con tanti saluti cordiali, Suo Voglia gradire i più cordiali saluti, Suo	} Sincerely yours, etc.
Mi creda (or Credetemi) con stima Il Suo (Vostro) aff^{mo5} amico Una stretta di mano dal Suo amico	} Cordially yours, etc.
Saluti cordiali dal tuo (amico) Saluti affettuosi dal tuo (amico)	} Best regards from your friend, etc.

18 gennaio 19— Spett.[6] Ditta Bianchi e Martini Via Mazzini 52 16100 Genova	January 18, 19— Messrs. Bianchi, Martini & Co. 52 Mazzini Street Genoa 16100
Signori[7],	Gentlemen:
Vi[8] prego di spedirmi (or inviarmi) quanto prima (or al più presto possibile) a grande velocità (a piccola velocità, a volta di posta) quanto segue:	Please send me as soon as possible by express (by freight, by return mail) the following:
Favorite addebitarmi per l'importo di questa ordina- zione.	Please charge the amount of this order to my account.
Con distinti saluti	Yours truly

[5] Abbreviated from **affezionat**i**ssimo**. **Devot**i**ssimo** is also abbreviated to **dev**^{mo}. **pregiat**i**ssimo** to **pregiat.**^{mo}, **stimat**i**ssimo** to **stimat.**^{mo}, and **gentil**i**ssimo** to **gentil.** ^{mo}. [6] **Spett.** is the abbreviated form of **spett**a**bile**, *honorable*. **Ditta** = *Firm*. [7] In business letters the salutation is usually omitted. [8] In business letters the **Voi** form of address is customary.

Egregio Signore,

Siamo in possesso della pregiata Vostra (lettera) del 18 corr.[9] Eseguiremo la Vostra ordinazione con la massima attenzione. Vi mandiamo separatamente il nostro catalogo.

Nella speranza di nuovi ordini, con distinta stima

Vi salutiamo

Dear Sir:

We have received your letter of the 18th (of this month). Your order will have our best attention.

Under separate cover we are sending you our catalogue. Hoping to receive further orders, we remain.

Yours faithfully,

UN INVITO

La signora A sarebbe obbligatissima al signor B se la domenica sera del diciotto corr. alle otto, volesse recarsi da lei a cena.

AN INVITATION

Mrs. A requests the pleasure of Mr. B's company Sunday evening, (August) eighteenth, at eight o'clock, for supper.

RISPOSTA AFFERMATIVA

Il signor B ringrazia la signora A, ed è lieto di potere accettare il suo gentile invito.

ACCEPTANCE

Mr. B accepts with pleasure the kind invitation of Mrs. A.

RISPOSTA NEGATIVA

Il signor B è dolente che un impegno anteriore gli impedisca di accettare il gentile invito della signora A.

REGRETS

Mr. B is very sorry that a previous engagement prevents him from accepting the kind invitation which Mrs. A extends to him.

---

[9] **corr.** (or **c.m.**) = **corrente mese**, *this month.* Compare: **p.p.** = **prossimo passato** (**u.s.** = **ultimo scorso**), *ult.*; **p.v.** = **prossimo venturo**, *next.*

81. Parole d'augurio

Buon Natale!
Felice Capo d'Anno!
Buone Feste!
Buona Pasqua!
Buon compleanno!
Buon onomastico!
Buone vacanze!
Buon appetito!

Grazie, altrettanto.
Buon viaggio!
Buon divertimento!
Buona fortuna!
Benvenuto!
Cento di questi giorni!

Felicitazioni!
Salute!

Expressions of Greeting

Merry Christmas!
A Happy New Year!
Season's Greetings!
Happy Easter!
A happy birthday!
A happy Saint's Day![10]
Have a nice vacation!
(May you have a good appetite!)
Thank you, same to you.
Bon voyage!
Have a good time!
Good luck!
Welcome!
Many happy returns (of the day).
Congratulations!
God bless you! (when someone sneezes) and Here's to your health! (in drinking wine, etc.)

[10] In Italy one's saint's day is celebrated as much as, if not more than, one's birthday.

ESERCIZI

EXERCISES

Rispondete alle domande seguenti. *Answer the following questions.* (As is explained in the Preface, no diacritical marks are used in this section).

Scambiando saluti
1. Come sta Lei, signorina?
2. Come sta la signora Bianchi?
3. Anche Giovanni sta bene?
4. Non sta troppo bene Lei, signor...?
5. ArrivederLa, signorina!

Parla italiano Lei?
1. È italiano Lei, signor...?
2. Sono americano (-a) io, signorina...?
3. Lei parla inglese, signorina?
4. Anche io parlo inglese?
5. Lei è russo, signor...?

Ha un fiammifero?
1. Lei fuma, signor...?

2. Capisce, signor...? Parlo adagio, ca-pi-sce?
3. Dove posso comprare un pacchetto di sigarette?
4. Ha un fiammifero, signorina?
5. Arrivederci!

Una lettera
1. Lei scrive lettere?
2. Quante lettere scrive Lei?
3. Che francobolli vuole Lei?
4. Ecco la Sua penna, signorina! Grazie!
5. Dov'è la buca per le lettere?

La famiglia
1. Lei scrive spesso a Sua madre?
2. Scrive anche a Suo fratello?
3. È a Nuova York il Suo amico?
4. Che cosa fa il Suo amico a Nuova York?
5. Lei, signorina, che cosa studia?

Il tempo
1. Fa freddo oggi?
2. Fa brutto tempo nell'estate?
3. Quando piove molto?
4. È sempre la migliore stagione l'autunno?
5. Quando fa bel tempo?

L'ora
1. È l'una e mezzo ora?
2. Che ore sono ora, signor...?
3. Quando è l'una e venti è anche l'una e mezzo?
4. Quando sono le tre meno dieci, mancano...alle tre.
5. Quando mancano venti minuti alle otto, sono le otto e...

La presentazione
1. Mi permetta di presentarLe la signorina Neri corrisponde (*corresponds*) a...
2. Piacere di fare la Sua conoscenza corrisponde a...
3. Signor . . . , Le presento il signor...

4. Signorina . . . , Le presento la signorina...
5. Piacere di aver fatto la Sua conoscenza, signorina!

Va in Italia?
1. Buon giorno, signor . . . , come va oggi?
2. Che cosa c'è di nuovo, signorina...?
3. Parla italiano Lei?
4. Dove ha studiato l'italiano Lei?
5. L'ha dimenticato o lo parla?

Buon viaggio
1. Quando parte il nostro amico (*our friend*) per l'Italia?
2. Perchè ripassa la grammatica il nostro amico?
3. Il mese prossimo corrisponde a...
4. Va in Italia o in piroscafo il nostro amico?
5. Viaggerà con degli amici?

L'agenzia di viaggi
1. Quando partono gli aviogetti dell'*Alitalia* per Roma?
2. Lei, signorina, a che ora preferisce partire?
3. Arriva di sera a Roma l'aereo dell'*Alitalia*?
4. Quando Lei viaggia, signor . . . , viaggia sempre in prima classe?
5. Quando Lei paga il biglietto, paga in contanti?

Il viaggio in aeroplano
1. Che cosa non aveva veduto il signore che fumava all'aeroporto?
2. Quando un posto non è occupato diciamo (*we say*, from dire)...
3. Quando si allacciano le cinture i passeggeri (*passengers*)?
4. Sono i vuoti d'aria che causano i tuffi in un aereo?
5. Perchè il signore in aereo vuole dormire un po'?

L'atterraggio e la dogana
1. Il signore prende (*takes*) il caffellatte?
2. Che cosa vedono (*see*) dall'aereo?
3. Ha qualche cosa da dichiarare il signore?

4. Quante sigarette dichiara?
5. Perchè va (*goes*, from andare) all'ufficio di cambio?

Il tassì

1. Il signore va all'albergo in autobus?
2. Come vuole arrivare all'albergo?
3. Perchè si preoccupa il signore?
4. È lontano dalle porte della città l'albergo?
5. Cosa domanda (*asks*) il signore quando arrivano all'albergo?

L'albergo

1. Il signore desidera una camera a due letti?
2. Che cosa vorrebbe (*would like*, from volere)?
3. Che cosa c'è nel bagno?
4. Perchè non importa che non c'è l'aria condizionata?
5. Che cosa scriviamo sul modulo di registrazione?
6. Perchè telefona il signore?
7. Che cosa dice (*says*, from dire)?
8. Perchè la cameriera domanda se il signore desidera più coperte?
9. Che cosa desidera e perchè?
10. Perchè la cameriera vuole portare un'altra bottiglia d'acqua minerale?

La biancheria

1. Perchè il signore chiama la cameriera?
2. Perchè non c'è fretta?
3. Lei preferisce i colletti delle Sue camicie inamidati, signor...?
4. Chi (*Who*) stirerà i pantaloni?
5. A che ora vuole essere svegliato (*awakened*) il signore?

In giro per Roma

1. Che cosa chiamano per andare a visitare le catacombe?
2. Lei ha mai visitato la chiesa di San Pietro?
3. Dov'è la Cappella Sistina?

4. Di che cosa è piena Roma?
5. Chi aspetta la guida?

Davanti a un'edicola
1. Che cos'è Il *Messaggero*?
2. Conosceva il *Rome Daily American* la signora?
3. Chi compra questo giornale?
4. Ci sono sempre molti turisti a Roma?
5. Vuole soltanto (*only*) il giornale del mattino la signora?

Il tram e l'autobus
1. Passa ogni venti minuti il tram che va al parco?
2. Perchè non possono salire in tram?
3. Soltanto il tram va al parco?
4. Lei, signorina, preferisce il tram o l'autobus? Perchè?
5. Ci sono autobus nella nostra città?

Al museo
1. C'è un museo nella nostra città? Dov'è ?
2. È aperto tutta la giornata (*day*) il museo?
3. Quando è gratis l'entrata ai musei in Italia?
4. Si paga anche la guida? Perchè?
5. Che cosa vendono dentro al museo?

Alla banca
1. Che cosa deve (from dovere) mostrare il signore per cambiare un assegno?
2. Perchè era peccato?
3. È sempre lo stesso (*same*) il cambio?
4. Chi vuole aprire un conto alla Banca Commerciale?
5. Che interesse (*interest*) danno le banche della nostra città?

Giorni festivi
1. Perchè era chiuso l'ufficio postale?
2. È vero che la Repubblica Italiana è più vecchia della Repubblica degli Stati Uniti d'America?

3. Quali (*Which*) feste americane non corrispondono alle feste nazionali italiane?
4. Quali feste italiane non corrispondono alle feste americane?
5. Perchè non c'è pericolo di essere investiti da una macchina nelle città italiane il giorno di Ferragosto?

Il telefono

1. Dove troviamo un elenco telefonico?
2. Quando un italiano risponde al telefono, qual è la prima parola che dice?
3. Che cosa aspettava il signor Moretti?
4. Cosa dice Robert Martin quando non sente?
5. Perchè non sente niente?

Macchine fotografiche e accessori

1. Quante fotografie vuole il signore?
2. Compra del film?
3. È riuscita bene una fotografia che è sfocata?
4. Perchè non possono (from potere) accomodare la macchina subito?
5. Che cosa compra il signore?

Al ristorante

1. Lei, signor . . . , come preferisce le uova?
2. Lei ha mangiato mai il prosciutto italiano? È differente dal prosciutto americano?
3. Lei che cosa beve (from bere) a colazione?
4. Signorina . . . , descriva la colazione che Lei preferisce!
5. Che cosa c'è nel coperto?
6. Perchè i due signori vanno (from andare) in quel ristorante?
7. Prima di tutto che cosa vogliono (from volere) vedere?
8. Che cosa preferisce mangiare Lei con il pollo arrosto?
9. Ordiniamo (*do we order*) l'acqua minerale in un ristorante americano?
10. Erano fresche le pere?

Autonoleggio
1. Che cosa desidera il signore?
2. È possibile noleggiare una macchina nella nostra città? Dove?
3. Perchè noleggia un'automobile il signore?
4. Che cosa è necessario mostrare per noleggiare una macchina?
5. Quando abbiamo bisogno di una carta stradale?

Il viaggio in automobile
1. Quando andiamo a una stazione di servizio?
2. Corrisponde al "gallon" americano il litro?
3. È sufficiente controllare soltanto la benzina prima di partire per un lungo viaggio?
4. Lei preferisce guidare (to drive) in una strada a due carreggiate o in un'autostrada?
5. Merita sempre conto prendere un'autostrada?

In viaggio
1. È vero che le strade più corte sono sempre le più belle?
2. Sono tutte in buono stato le strade del nostro stato (State)?
3. Sa Lei dov'è Sorrento?
4. Le piace (do you like) guidare quando ci sono molte curve?
5. Che cosa è bene fare quando guidiamo in una strada con molte curve?

Il garage
1. Quando andiamo a un garage?
2. Lei, signor . . . , sa (do you know? from sapere) se la parola "candela" ha soltanto un significato (meaning)?
3. È più facile (easy) guidare in discesa o in salita?
4. Ci vuole molto tempo a imparare a guidare una macchina?
5. Costano molto le riparazioni di un'automobile?

Il viaggio in piroscafo
1. Lei ha mai viaggiato in un piroscafo? Dove?

2. Quando parte il piroscafo che va da Napoli a Palermo?
3. Perchè il signore va a un'agenzia di navigazione?
4. Perchè non ci sono più molti piroscafi fra gli Stati Uniti e l'Europa?
5. Lei, signorina, sa che cosa è un aliscafo?

Un giro per la Sicilia
1. Che cosa vorrebbe fare il signore a Palermo?
2. Come si può (*can one* from potere) fare il giro della Sicilia?
3. Che cosa gli consiglia il portiere dell'albergo?
4. Dove ci sono antichi templi greci in Sicilia?
5. Perchè è interessante fare un viaggio a Piazza Armerina?

In un caffè
1. Dove intende andare il signor Brown?
2. Perchè i due amici (*friends*) si fermano a un caffè?
3. Perchè preferiscono sedersi fuori?
4. Lei preferisce le paste o i gelati?
5. Che tempo fa oggi, signorina...?

Il viaggio in treno
1. Dove chiediamo (*do we ask*) informazioni in una stazione?
2. Prende il treno della mattina o della sera il signor Brown?
3. Arriva sempre alle diciassette il treno che parte per Firenze alle tredici?
4. Le piace (*do you like*) viaggiare in treno, signor...?
5. Perchè è utile (*useful*) un orario?

La biglietteria
1. Quante classi ci sono in un treno italiano?
2. Ci sono soltanto biglietti di corsa semplice?
3. Perchè non compra un biglietto di andata e ritorno il signor Brown?
4. Costa più un biglietto di prima classe o di seconda classe?
5. Su che cosa c'è uno sconto?

L'ufficio di spedizione
1. Quando chiamiamo un facchino?
2. Quando abbiamo bisogno di un baule?
3. Ha un baule il signor Brown? Che cosa ha?
4. Perchè non deve pagare niente?
5. Perchè lascia l'indirizzo?

Nel deposito di bagagli
1. Dove lascia i bagagli?
2. È vero che il deposito chiude alle nove di sera?
3. Quando deve pagare per depositare i bagagli?
4. Perchè non deve perdere gli scontrini?
5. Ha soltanto una chiave per ogni valigia?

Sul marciapiede della stazione
1. Perchè deve fare presto il signor Brown?
2. Quali posti sono migliori per osservare il paesaggio?
3. Quando salgono (*from* salire) in treno i due signori?
4. Che cosa mettiamo sul portabagagli dello scompartimento?
5. È permesso fumare in tutti gli scompartimenti?

In treno
1. È possibile sporgersi dal finestrino in un treno americano?
2. Quando entra la polvere nello scompartimento di un treno?
3. C'è l'aria condizionata soltanto nei treni?
4. Che cosa fa il controllore?
5. Quando Lei ha fame in un treno, che cosa fa?

Oggetti perduti
1. Quando andiamo all'ufficio degli Oggetti Perduti?
2. Perchè è bene avere un cartellino nelle valige?
3. C'era tutto nella valigia del signor Brown?
4. Aveva molto denaro (*money*) in tasca?
5. Quando gli disse (from dire) di ritornare l'impiegato (*clerk*)?

Il Palio di Siena
1. Che cosa è il Palio, signorina...?
2. Lei sa in che parte d'Italia è Siena?
3. Quando ha luogo (*takes place*) il Palio?
4. Che cosa c'è prima della corsa?
5. Che cosa sventolava sul Carroccio?

La lettera di raccomandazione
1. Quando abbiamo bisogno d'una lettera di raccomandazione?
2. Sono utili i biglietti da visita? Perchè?
3. Chi manda tanti saluti al signor Bianchi?
4. Come possiamo (from potere) dire invece di (*instead of*) "sono felicissimo di fare la Sua conoscenza?"
5. Qual è il Suo indirizzo signor...?

Affittando un appartamento
1. Come rispondiamo quando una persona dice "È permesso?"
2. Lei dove preferisce abitare (*to live*), al centro o in periferia? Perchè?
3. Quali sono le stanze principali d'un appartamento?
4. Che cosa c'è in una cucina?
5. E in una stanza da bagno che cosa c'è?

Nella libreria
1. C'è una libreria nella nostra città? Dov'è?
2. Lei legge molti romanzi? Quali romanzi preferisce?
3. Abbiamo premi letterari negli Stati Uniti?
4. Perchè è utile una pianta della città?
5. Perchè è utile un dizionario?

Nel negozio di scarpe
1. Perchè l'impiegato prende la misura al signore?
2. Quali sono le parti del piede?
3. Quando non sono comode le scarpe?

4. Quando vogliamo (from volere) far mettere i tacchi nuovi a un paio di scarpe, dove andiamo?
5. Perchè è utile il calzatoio?

Dal barbiere
1. Che cosa domanda il barbiere al signore?
2. Lei quando va dal (*to the*) barbiere?
3. Sono di moda i capelli corti oggi?
4. Gli lava i capelli il barbiere?
5. C'è un barbiere qui vicino?

Nel salone di bellezza
1. Deve fare un appuntamento la signorina?
2. Che cosa vuole prima di tutto?
3. Ci vuole (*does it take*) più tempo ad asciugare i capelli di un signore o di una signora?
4. Lavano soltanto i capelli in un salone di bellezza?
5. Che cosa compra la signorina?

Dal sarto
1. Lei che stoffa preferisce per i Suoi abiti?
2. Lei va da un sarto quando vuole comprare un abito?
3. Vuole descrivere il mio abito, signorina...?
4. Deve pagare subito il signore?
5. Che cosa dovrà (from dovere) fare venerdì?

Dalla sarta
1. Perchè la signora deve aspettare?
2. Le dispiace dovere aspettare?
3. Secondo (*according to*) la sarta, come le sta il vestito?
4. Era vero che il vestito le stava bene?
5. Potrà (from potere) mettersi il vestito quella sera la signora?

In un magazzino
1. Come si sale (*does one go up*) al terzo piano nel magazzino?
2. Dov'è il reparto tappeti?
3. Che cosa c'è a buon mercato?

4. Che sconto c'è sulle camicie?
5. Compra anche delle cravatte? Perchè?

In un'oreficeria

1. Quando non va bene un orologio?
2. È necessario caricare tutti i giorni anche un orologio elettrico?
3. Se non merita conto accomodare un orologio, che cosa facciamo?
4. Che cosa compra la signorina?
5. Compra subito la collana di perle la signorina? Perchè?

Alla posta

1. Quanto costa l'affrancatura d'una lettera per l'interno negli Stati Uniti ora?
2. E una lettera per l'estero quanto costa?
3. Che cosa scriviamo su una busta?
4. Dopo che abbiamo scritto (from scrivere) una lettera, che cosa facciamo (from fare)?
5. Se impostiamo una lettera oggi, quando arriva a Roma?
6. Che cosa non era giunto a Bologna?
7. Aveva la ricevuta il signore?
8. Perchè molti turisti vanno (from andare) al fermo in posta?
9. Che cosa dobbiamo (from dovere) mostrare all'impiegato?
10. Se il destinatario non è più allo stesso indirizzo, che cosa fa l'ufficio postale?

Dal medico

1. Quando chiamiamo il medico?
2. È vero che tutti i medici sono specialisti?
3. Perchè il dottore si fermerà soltanto un minuto?
4. Quando è necessario andare all'ospedale?
5. Stanno aperte tutta la notte le farmacie?

Dal dentista

1. È sempre necessario fissare un'ora prima di andare dal dentista?

2. Quali denti fanno soffrire molto?
3. Se in un dente c'è un buco piccolo, che cosa può fare il dentista?
4. Quali sono le migliori (*best*) otturazioni secondo Lei?
5. Las signorina dovrà ritornare dal dentista per un controllo?

In farmacia

1. Quando andiamo in una farmacia?
2. Quando prendiamo l'aspirina?
3. Lei è raffreddata ora, signorina...?
4. Quando non piacciono le pasticche ai bambini?
5. Che differenza c'è fra (*between*) le farmacie italiane e le farmacie americane?

Ferragosto

1. Perchè a quel signore consigliano di non andare a Venezia il quindici di agosto?
2. Quando fa caldo in Italia?
3. Che cosa fanno le persone che hanno lavorato tutto l'anno?
4. Lei dove preferisce andare in vacanza? Perchè?
5. Chi resta nelle città italiane a Ferragosto?

Il viaggio a Venezia

1. Quale città è la Regina dell'Adriatico? Perchè?
2. Perchè il signore non si tratterrà a lungo a Venezia?
3. Che cosa unisce Venezia alla terra ferma?
4. Che cosa vede nel Canal Grande?
5. Perchè non visita subito la Basilica di San Marco?

Al Lido

1. Quando è una giornata ideale per andare al Lido?
2. Perchè non vanno al Lido in gondola?
3. Lei sa il nome di qualche altra spiaggia italiana?
4. Le piace nuotare, signorina. ...? Dove?
5. Quando c'è caso di bruciarsi?
6. Dove vanno a mettersi le mutandine?

7. Perchè devono (from dovere) fare attenzione a non prendere troppo sole?
8. Quando sono utili le pinne?
9. Lei sa nuotare, signor ...? Quando ha imparato?
10. Che cosa c'è nello stabilimento balneare?

Il cinema

1. Lei ha mai veduto un film italiano? Quale?
2. È vero che i biglietti del cinema costano poco oggi?
3. Perchè i due amici prendono il tassì per andare al cinema?
4. Perchè uno dei due amici pesta il piede a una signora?
5. Di che cosa aveva voglia uno dei due amici?

L'esposizione di pitture

1. Ci sono esposizioni di pitture nella nostra città? Dove?
2. Perchè la signora (il signore) non conosce le vie della città?
3. Lei che tipo di pitture preferisce?
4. È bella soltanto l'arte classica?
5. Che cos'è un affresco?
6. Lei preferisce un quadro a olio o un acquerello?
7. Che cos'è un'occasione?
8. Perchè quel quadro faceva (from fare) venire l'acquolina in bocca?
9. Chi aveva un'espressione feroce negli occhi?
10. Perchè il pittore (*painter*) non voleva vendere il quadro per diecimila lire?

Il teatro dell'opera

1. C'erano ancora molti biglietti per l'opera?
2. Lei è andato (-*a*) mai a un'opera?
3. Lei preferisce le opere o le sinfonie? Perchè?
4. Quando Lei va all'opera che biglietti compra?
5. Che cos'è il "libretto?" Chi lo sa?
6. Le piace mettersi (*to wear*) lo smoking, signor...?
7. Chi è la maschera?
8. Perchè molte persone portano (*take*) il binocolo all'opera?

9. Quando si alza il sipario?
10. A Lei piace più la voce del tenore o la voce del soprano?

Natale

1. È soprattutto una festa religiosa il Natale negli Stati Uniti?
2. Che cosa fanno gli Americani a Natale?
3. Lei manda molte lettere per Natale?
4. È vero che i bambini italiani in generale ricevono i regali il giorno di Natale?
5. Che cosa fa la Befana?
6. Che cosa fanno molti italiani la settimana di Natale?
7. Che cosa è il Presepio?
8. Che cosa fanno i ragazzi in alcune famiglie?
9. Le piacerebbe (*would you like*) essere in Italia per Natale?
10. Che cosa è il torrone?

Attraverso L'Italia

1. Che cosa farà il signore a Milano?
2. Perchè vale la pena visitare Padova?
3. Dov'è la Valle del Po?
4. Dove vanno gl'Italiani per gli sport invernali?
5. A Lei piace sciare? Dove va a sciare?

La visita d'addio

1. Perchè va dal (*calls on*) signor Nardi il signor Brown?
2. Che cosa non dimenticherà mai?
3. Si è divertito a Venezia? Perchè?
4. Che cosa dice il signor Nardi al signor Brown?
5. Quando Lei andrà in Italia, che cosa vorrà (from *volere*) visitare?

INDEX TO APPENDIX